NO MORE SOLDIERING

NO MORE SOLDIERING

Conscientious Objectors in the First World War

Stephen Wade

AMBERLEY

This book is dedicated to the memory of one of the most heroic individuals of the First World War. His name has no medal of glory attached to it and he has so far been forgotten in mainstream history.

To Alex Peddieson, who died at Red Roses Camp, Carmarthen, in an epidemic of influenza, collapsing while nursing his comrades.

First published 2016

Amberley Publishing
The Hill, Stroud
Gloucestershire, GL5 4EP

www.amberley-books.com

Copyright © Stephen Wade, 2016

The right of Stephen Wade to be identified as the Author of this work has been asserted in accordance with the Copyrights, Designs and Patents Act 1988.

ISBN 978 1 4456 4894 1 (paperback)
ISBN 978 1 4456 4895 8 (ebook)

British Library Cataloguing in Publication Data. A catalogue record for this book is available from the British Library.

Typesetting and Origination by Amberley Publishing
Printed in the UK.

CONTENTS

AUTHOR'S NOTE: ABBREVIATIONS

For convenience, in the main text of the book, after the introductory sections, I will use the following abbreviations, as the people and groups to which they refer are prominent in my biographies and are often repeated:

CO – Conscientious Objector
DORA – Defence of the Realm Act, 1914
FAU – Friends Ambulance Unit
ILP – Independent Labour Party
NCF – No-Conscription Fellowship

PRELUDE: TWO STORIES OF MEN WHO WOULD NOT FIGHT

In Cleethorpes

James Brightmore, a Manchester man, was at the seaside at one time during the First World War, but not for ice creams and sandcastles.

He found himself in the Council House at Cleethorpes in July 1917, for refusing to obey an order. He had already suffered such ignominy that his case had reached Parliament and some officers involved had retired. In June of that year he had refused to assemble his equipment, and witnesses from the Army had testified to that effect. He argued that the order was illegal and indeed 'unusual'.

Earlier that year he had been sentenced to nine months in Lincoln prison (reduced to six later) for an offence 'committed as a conscientious objector'. From that point there had been a campaign against him, lasting from the January up to his appearance in July. First he was asked to pick up waste paper and refused; he was given twenty-three days' solitary confinement and his officer had said to him, 'I'll make it so damned uncomfortable for you, that you will be glad to start soldiering for your own protection.' A reign of terror began.

His tormentor, Captain McBean, said, 'Give him Devonport rations and let him cook them himself. Put him among the Expeditionary Force men but don't let him mix with them. He isn't fit to associate with soldiers. Cut his buttons and badges off … he is a disgrace to them.' It is not clear whether the officer meant by 'Devonport rations' that the man should be tied up, or whether he simply meant meagre food, as implied by the old myth about 'Debon's share', meaning the very worst leftovers – but whatever his meaning, a terrible and hateful regime of punishment began against Brightmore.

The victim was taken to a hole which had been dug to a depth of 4 feet and he was left to stand there; later it was deepened to 7 feet. He was left there, and he refused food. The next day the hole was deepened and he had to remain there; he was soon standing in water. Brightmore's account was:

> I spent most of the day in the hole, water accumulating until it was ankle-deep. I refused food that day. Next morning, 30 June, they came and took another two feet of mud and clay out of the hole. I found my strength failing and ate some bread and margarine. It rained and I was wet through but at night a corporal let me out and let me sleep in a marquee.

The corporal was severely reprimanded for his act of humanity. The punishment continued. The officer provided a piece of wood for the victim to stand on: a pathetic attempt to limit the suffering, but it was no help. Then Brightmore was hauled before a medical officer.

By that time Brightmore was becoming more determined to take on his tormentor and be uncooperative whenever he could, so he refused the medical inspection. The officer did not enforce the examination, so the doctor merely looked at the prisoner and said he looked fit. He was then passed as fit. After eating some beans and meat, another day passed in the hole. Again one man let him go to the marquee, and again he was sent back to the hole. He was left in the water, at the bottom of the hole, for another four days, in the bitter east wind. He said, 'During Thursday night I dozed a bit, but my limbs ached so that I could not sleep. I was in a state of collapse by morning, and asked to see a doctor.'

It is amazing to read that Brightmore was then taken before a senior officer, still in his soaking clothes. He was asked if he had any cause for complaints and he chose that moment to go through the awful treatment he had received; the only effect that had was that he was taken to the guard tent rather than the hole, still in his wet clothes.

The real bone of contention was that Brightmore insisted that a conscientious objector should not be treated as a soldier. This escalated the situation when McBean asked to see him and told him that he would be treated as a soldier. At that interview, the poor man had been in the hole for eleven days. It was not long after that he refused to assemble his equipment, not defining himself as 'a soldier'. Standing in the court in July, he said again that he could not be punished for a military offence, since he was not a soldier.

McBean had become seriously ill by this time, and he came to the enquiry from his sickbed in Leeds. Brightmore had known this and had asked for an adjournment so that his torturer could attend. It was clearly a case of a battle of wills and a sense of deep injustice. The military hearing could not decide on a course of action and the case dragged on. It had to end in an impasse, and so it did, being deferred with no decision. In the end, the only course of action was to remove McBean from the situation, and that naturally resolved matters; but the story is one of the worst cases of cruelty against a conscientious objector in those terrible years, when to be given 'the white feather' was a disgrace, and when intellectuals and activists were imprisoned for their political views. Brightmore must have been longing to be home in Manchester, where he probably would have preferred a stretch in Strangeways to any more time with McBean in Cleethorpes.

This experience was not rare. Such suffering was happening across the land, all in the name of patriotism. It is hard to forget Dr Samuel Johnson's definition of patriotism when we read about Brightmore: 'The last refuge of a scoundrel.'

From York Barracks to Ripon Camp

Ernest England was a Quaker from Leeds. Despite being classified as medically unfit for military service, he was not left alone when the Military Service Act came into force in January 1916. He was recalled and put into Army custody. So began a sad tale of mother and son, leading to one of the most inhuman and tragic deaths in the story of resistance to war. As Ernest was taken to York Barracks, his mother, who had been with him up to that point, was taken ill. A few days later, the son was told that his mother was very seriously ill and was dying. He was given no compassionate leave by the immediate authorities, but a family member took the extreme step of phoning the brigadier general of the regiment, and Ernest was given permission. He was by that time at Ripon Camp, and his only means of getting to Leeds was by taxi. He arrived at his mother's side just a few hours before she passed away. He stayed for her funeral, but then in June 1917 he was sent to Wormwood Scrubs.

Then begins his slow decline. Ernest was weak; he had a serious illness himself, but was still put to hard work. He was then transferred to Knutsford, where there was a workshop, but before long he was on the move again, first to Wakefield and then to Dartmoor. The first historian of the NCF takes up the story: 'His letters from Dartmoor show him shivering with cold, working in the snow with wet feet, and suffering from the diet … after a day of hard shovel work, tea consisted of a thick slice of bread, a scrape of margarine and a mug of tea … Six weeks later his enfeebled frame succumbed to influenza at home on 6 March 1919.'

INTRODUCTION

This is an account of the experiences of those who, in the First World War, would not directly fight against the German army and their allies; those who would participate in a non-combatant role, and those who would take no action at all to further the cause of a militaristic enterprise intended to take the lives of enemy people. The main element in the biographical profiles will be an account of the latter class – the so-called absolutists. However, before beginning the narrative of these men and women who held to their pacifist principles, a survey is necessary, introducing several contextual factors which lie behind the stories of the people in focus.

The Photograph Album

It was found during the normal process of research: an imperial-size bound collection of white card sheets with a front page which read, 'Photographs of Prison Life, by a Conscientious Objector – Percy Smith *c.* 1916.' At first I didn't notice that it had, in fact, never been published; it was an item from a private archive. It certainly invited the reader to turn the pages, and so I did. There followed a shock. The pictures were from inside the prison walls of institutions such as Dartmoor, Wakefield and Knutsford. In the last venue there had been one of the most violent confrontations between the public and the objectors in the chronicles of the peace movement of the First World War.

The pictures included a man being flogged, prisoners in workshops, and, to my amazement, there was a photograph labelled 'the insanity testing box'. This showed what is best described as a coffin stood on end. There was more: a picture of a man on the floor of 'the padded cell' at Wakefield, his hands on his head as if about to scream. Finally, in total contrast, there was a picture showing a richly decorated gift book with a card alongside, both bearing the name Charles William Hunt. 'Dear Sir, as a mark of the high regard and respect we, the men who have been employed at the Knutsford Work Centre, hold you, we ask you to accept this address.'

What greater contrast could there be than this? Here we have images of the very worst of punishments handed out to those who would not fight the enemy, mixed with what was clearly a tribute to a man in charge of the workshop who had shown humanity and consideration with regard to his charges. This remarkable contrast is to be evident throughout the following biographies. My responses on first reading this document were, understandably, best described as indignation and revulsion. Man's inhumanity to man has rarely been better exemplified than in the pictures gathered by Percy Smith.

I have not been able to find out anything about Mr Smith; there appears to be nothing in print about him in the publications on conscientious objection. But the collection he put together makes the maximum impact on the reader today – as, of course, he intended. Yet there is that redemptive little card, a testimony to something that sustained the brave men who had faced prison for long stretches, along with the hatred and abuse of the men around them who had answered the call to arms and who had been taught how to kill with bullets and bayonets.

Percy Smith, by whatever means we will never know, created a document which tells a story through pictures – one that is very hard to accept, but it stands there, as a record of abuse and brutality.

It is this kind of material dimension on great events that directs the historian to see the truths of the altogether human experience caught up within the overarching generalised story that tends to be generated and handed down. Looking at those pictures, the cruelty of those who could not understand a man's choice not to take another life comes across far more strikingly than it does in a thousand academic texts. Nevertheless, there has been a growing literature on the conscientious objectors of the First World War, as hindsight and broader studies of the reasons for that conflict have emerged.

The Background

A survey of the content of the popular newspaper *The Daily Graphic* in 1890 makes it clear that over twenty years before the First World War broke out in August 1914, Britain had a powerful preoccupation with military life and affairs. The major features concern the military summer manoeuvres, the activities of rifle clubs, the marches of the volunteer regiments, marches of quasi-military groups of all kinds in the streets across the land, accounts of the Prussian-invented 'War Game' and countless other events related to the Army. On top of this there was the obsession with naval power in the 1890s, when the German navy was being developed to try to compete with the British, which had ruled the seas and preserved the British Empire for centuries.

It was a reflection of a total ideological commitment to war and empire as a state of mind as well as a state of being. The date 1890 may seem a long way from the imagery of the trenches we now have in our minds when the First World War is mentioned, but it has to be recalled that between the 1880s, when Britain crushed the revolt of nationalists in Egypt, and 1898, when Kitchener was victorious at Omdurman over the Mahdist state, it seemed to most that the great enterprise of consolidating the Eastern Empire and African territory was possible, and that the great rival Germany could still be kept at bay, as long as the military attitude prevailed.

In the decades before 1914, the only enigma for the modern reader on this subject is that, after the near defeat and massive loss of life in the Anglo-Boer Wars (1899–1902), soldiering and its rigid class structures remained unchanged and imperial ideologies stayed firmly in place.

Consequently, when the shadow of a war on a much grander scale was cast over Europe in the later Edwardian years, the authorities saw the need for the enforcement of the ideal of sacrifice for one's country. The story of those who said no to soldiering in this context begins with that mindset of 'Tommy Atkins' and his idealistic narrative in popular culture. In very recent memoir literature of the First World War, participants have assessed their feelings before, during and after the conflict. Ronald Skirth, for instance, in his 2010 book *The Reluctant Tommy,* locates his dissent to a crisis at Etaples in which he refused to follow an order and threw down his gun. That was a capital offence, and the statistics show that 346 men were hanged or shot between 1914 and 1920 for cowardice, desertion and related offences. Skirth was fortunate, but his testimony explains the source of much conscientious objection: the epiphany of seeing the futility of killing which emerged after an encounter with the corpse of a young German soldier. 'On 8 June, 1917 war for me changed from being an abstraction to a personal problem ... I would have to live my life with a troubled conscience ... My adolescence ended that day. Henceforward I had to live and think as an adult.'

Skirth's words explain very powerfully the core of belief and empathy which lies deep inside the being of conscientious objectors.

*

Readers today – a century after that summer of 1914, when most thought that the war would end by Christmas and when the horrors of the trenches were as yet unknown – are subject to the accumulated influence of thousands of books, films, radio programmes and poems showing the horrors of battle in this 'new' kind of conflict. Yet in the end that narrative is still planted in our minds as one of heroes, of noble sacrifice, of poppies and war memorials; the story we are told repeatedly is that of brave men and women facing up to the likelihood of death, day after day, month after month and year after year. Only in the tiniest interstices of that epic tale do we find the stories of other people, the ones who said, 'No, I will not take the life of a fellow human being.'

In 1914, the media made it clear that the war was for the professionals; everyday workers, young students and men working to maintain young families never gave a moment's thought to the possibility that they would one day be told to be soldiers. *Told* is the operative word. Throughout the long history of the British Empire, the fighting against the Indian peoples, the Ashanti, the Zulus, Napoleon's French and the Russians in the Crimea had been done by the professional soldier: the Tommy Atkins that Kipling had celebrated as the scrapper, hardened in a hundred battles, wearing his red coat proudly and risking his life while the collier, the farmer and the domestic servant went on maintaining the status quo back home. Then, after the shock of massive failure as the British Expeditionary Force met defeat after defeat in 1915, Lord Kitchener and the other top brass of the Army wanted more men – men who were not soldiers – and thousands upon thousands had to meet what many later called 'The Test' of their manhood and patriotism.

As massive numbers of ordinary men went to make an attestation in late 1915, they still thought that the day when they put on a uniform and carried a gun would not come. They were asked to 'attest', which meant simply stating that they would be willing to fight if needed. But then, there were still plenty of soldiers, surely?

Then, in January 1916, the Military Service Act was passed, making it clear that the government wanted men for the great war machine that was set up and digging in across the Channel, in a war that was going to last for some time, perhaps beyond many another Christmas.

The following stories of those who became labelled COs (conscientious objectors) start with an account of the first united front of resistance in Wales, a mix of socialists and Christians. After that the focus switches to look at the lives and experiences of those who refused to fight – whether their attitude was simply that they would not go to war at all, or that they would do other, secondary duties, as long as they were not taking the lives of other human beings.

The biographies gathered here include tales of prison experience, the ordeal of facing a tribunal in front of those who thought they were staring at a coward, the experience of being shunned and reviled by all those in the community who believed in the 'just' war taking place on the Western Front, the test of their Christian resolve and, perhaps above all, the tough confrontation with their individual inner beliefs, which were now being tested by reality.

What for most had been the substance of a stirring sermon or religious tract, a powerful hymn or a resounding psalm, was now a hard fact of their reality; the question they faced was whether every war was immoral and wrong, or if this specific war was different in some way. Were there exceptions to the thinking of pacifism and Christian belief? After all, the newspapers of 1914 and 1915 had made it clear to all that the German army raging across France and Belgium was committing terrible atrocities. Not only were Germans supposedly raping and pillaging in Belgium, but there were reputedly German spies everywhere in Britain. There had been reports of spies at all the major docks, including Cardiff and Swansea, and anyone with a German name was likely to be attacked and their property destroyed. This was made worse by an event in the Irish Sea shortly before men had to 'attest' their war readiness.

In May 1915 the liner *Lusitania* was sunk by a German submarine after sailing out of Liverpool. The outrage after this was savage and irrational. Anything German in the land was hated, and shopkeepers with German names had their property smashed and were attacked if they walked out in the street. *The Weekly Dispatch* wrote, 'How many Germans are living in this country and are not in gaol?'

In Liverpool, as Pat O'Mara has written, 'On the corner of Scotland Road ominous gangs were gathering.' The reason was that many of the dead were from that area. O'Mara recalled hearing the cries and moans of people around the Scotland Road area who had lost loved ones in the disaster. In Bostock Street almost every home had blinds or curtains drawn closed as a sign of a death. The men who had died were mostly Irish coal-trimmers, sailors and firemen from the ship. Mr Taylor, who had been a steward on Cunard ships, recalled that on the day after the disaster there were photographs of bodies in the basement of a building in Rumford Street. He noted, 'One I particularly remember of a young woman lying with her baby in her arms, but many of the photographs were too horrible for words.'

The gangs were out to beat up anyone who might be considered to be German, so that included anyone with an un-English or vaguely European name. Properties with German links were naturally prime targets. While the gangs were out dozens of shops were attacked and police in the city made sixty-seven arrests. Later, Liverpool Corporation was to receive over five hundred compensation claims from residents.

*

As some of my stories will recall, at the very heart of the conscription regime was a Welshman, the most famous of his day, David Lloyd George. He had found it essential to back the conscription drive because of sheer necessity and his allegiance to the dominant ideology around him. In Wales there were around 1,000 COs, out of the British total of 16,500, so the proportion was high. However, as historians have often pointed out, 280,000 Welshmen served in the war years.

The following tales are of the principal combatants in this other war: they may not have squatted in stinking trenches and faced snipers' bullets, but they faced implacable opposition in the very heart of the place they had always called home. To be a CO in 1916 was to strive against a current as strong as the mightiest river. The Reverend Harding Rees, for instance, brought up in Llangennech, was destined to be sent to a work camp in Ireland. Of all the voices against death and destruction in the First World War, he recognised the nature of what was really opposing him; after watching trees felled in great numbers, and seeing there a metaphor of loss and death, he wrote, 'All this insatiable rapacity was the result of war which can only leave a blight on all things and a curse.'

Many of the lives recalled here give witness to the depths of suffering imposed upon those who dared to stand against the common consensus. In many cases this suffering was perhaps equal in deprivation and pain to anything experienced on the Western Front, as in this statement about a CO kept in prison, given in a parliamentary debate in November 1917, in response to a question from Mr Philip Snowden:

> This man, having persistently refused work, was given dietary punishment for six weeks by the visiting committee of Pentonville prison and fourteen days confinement to his cell. I know of no reason for remitting this punishment.

In fact the prisoner, William Hall, was not working because he did not see himself as a criminal. Back in the early nineteenth century the Rebecca Rioters and the Newport Chartists had argued the same – they were imprisoned because of their beliefs and not because of any criminal action.

We have to conclude that the level of suffering caused by fourteen days in solitary confinement, with nothing but bread and water, compares to many trench warfare experiences.

No More Soldiering brings to light the stories of the people who refused to kill the enemy. Were they cowards, or were they heroes of peace? The majority of people in 1916 knew exactly where they stood on the issue, but what about today? The jury may always be out on such acts of pacifism, but there is no doubting the courage of the people who kept to their values: from intellectuals such as T. H. Parry-Williams and T. Gwynn Jones, to long-term prisoner George Maitland Davies. They proved the maxim that 'the unexamined life is not worth living' and Milton's famous lines, 'Peace hath her victories / No less renowned than war.'

A Just War: Thoughtless Attitudes

In August 1914, a few weeks into the war, a certain Owen Deed wrote this letter to *The Malvern Gazette*:

> Sir, I am curious to know what has been the response of the young men of Malvern to our country's appeal? We know that our gallant Territorials have volunteered for the front, but there are hundreds of others whose one object is to let others bear the brunt while they seem to take a pride in shirking their responsibilities. Let one walk along the Belle Vue Terrace on Sunday evening. It cannot be that all have such great responsibilities at home which prevent them going. Is it that they are in a state of funk? If the latter they can still be of use. Why not start knitting meetings for these able-bodied young men or let them attend the women's working parties and hold wool

and thread needles? In any case let them be up and doing for their own sake, for Malvern's sake, for England's sake.

This was written in a climate of unthinking allegiance to an ingrained patriotic ethos, made more emotional and urgent by the reports of German atrocities in Belgium. While we now find it hard to forgive the sarcasm and narrow-minded references to the 'unnatural' femininity of male 'shirkers', there still remains the point that it was a just war, fought in accordance with an international pact, and, of course, that it was a war which might easily have led to a direct assault on Britain. The Zeppelin attacks on the east coast soon made it clear that the German navy was out to kill, maim and destroy.

There was undoubtedly a widespread acceptance of the need to make 'the sacrifice', and, as has been established by many historians, there was also a zeitgeist which expressed the notion of 'cleansing' in the furnace of war. Rupert Brooke's attitude was typical of many, as his biographer Nigel Jones notes: 'Squire asked him what all the rushing was for. "Well, if Armageddon is on," replied Brooke, "I suppose one should be there." Brooke also added, "There's a very bright sun and a lot of comedy in the world, so perhaps there's some point in my not getting shot. But also, there's a point in my getting shot."'

These strange, resigned attitudes, seemingly expressed without any really deep or searching questions being asked as to why one should take arms and enlist, are all the more strange when we consider the apparent satisfaction with the legislation which created the Territorial Force just a few years before 1914. In fact, a common attitude in the Edwardian years was expressed by one local historian writing on the theme of 'national security' in 1908:

Everybody must work, and everybody must be trained for home defence. We cannot abolish the Army, we must not violently disturb it, but we can by universal training gradually supersede or reduce it, and it will be no hardship to our youths on two nights in a week for two hours, or for four hours on a half-holiday, to go through exercises, with in summertime a fortnight's special drill and exercise, a part of which time to be spent in learning the use of tools, acts of agility ... whatever will tend to manliness ... such a course will lead to peace, not war.

If we compare this to the mighty and efficient Prussian war machine created after the Franco-Prussian War of 1870–71, with its extensive theories of warfare, love of strategic studies and organisational efficiency, then England seems distinctly amateurish and naive.

*

There is also the vexed question of the desire for peace. On 28 August 1913, the Peace Palace was opened on Carnegie Square, The Hague. It was funded by the philanthropist Andrew Carnegie, and in this introduction forms a cynical symbol: a palace of peace built at a time when the nations with imperial status or ambitions were spending more and more on arms and weaponry. People were well aware that technology was transmuting warfare; the Anglo-Boer Wars of 1899–1902 had shown that traditional strategies were no match for guerrilla war activity, and this had resulted in the impasse which eventually led to the concentration camps made by the British to hold the Boer families. There was an increasing sense that war was losing whatever semblance of gentlemanly conduct and morality it was once supposed to have had. The first international peace conference had been held at The Hague in 1899 and it had been decided there that a temple of peace should be constructed. A terrible irony hangs over that event now.

Before 1914, peace had been in the air across Europe for many years. In Britain, the thought of being forcibly conscripted into a war was diametrically opposed to the ideology of the nation. As John Sadler expressed it: 'For the British the idea of conscription was anathema: free men enlisted because it was right, not because the state compelled. Never before in history, and probably never again, was the road to war so heavily subscribed.' This thinking was expressed in a ditty:

> For we won't have conscription,
> We all hate conscription.
> We don't want conscription
> So we'll all be volunteers.

But the 'just war' thinking dominated, despite the theories and the resolves for peace. At certain moments in history, mass-will crushes individual moral values, and the latter tend to be engulfed, like a rock on a beach swallowed by the incoming tide. To be that rock, to maintain moral values which were previously untested, takes genuine and profound belief: are these cardboard cut-out ideals, or are they substantial, unwavering principles? The point is really that the test becomes one aimed directly at an individual's sole morality. This was powerfully expressed in Joachim Fest's *Not I: A German Childhood*, in which Joachim's father does precisely this: 'He put a piece of paper in front of each of us and dictated, "*etiam si omnes, ego non*" [as the others are, not I] "It's from the

Gospel according to St Mathew," he explained, "The scene on the Mount of Olives."'

The Law

Those who chose to stand against the majority and the 'fever' of the call to arms created a quandary for the lawmakers. To choose not to fight was to invite ridicule, abuse, humiliation and severe punishment. There was a likelihood that a CO would suffer something far worse than receiving a white feather; violence was always a threat as well as, of course, complete ostracism. It was assumed by patriots that a man who would not fight was accepting the domination of the enemy. This was so against the grain in the established ideology of a military, empire-directed race that it was a kind of treason, but whereas the Treason Acts – stretching back to 1351 – were based on the offender actually doing something against the life and domain of the sovereign, the new legislation of the First World War was intended to erase individual liberty of conscience and shift definitions in order to apply retribution to those very individuals who refused to commit an act.

The Shadow Still Exists

Finally, there is the element of shame. This lives on. The white feather presented by girls to the young men who would not or could not enlist was something beyond easy definition. It related to a notion of cowardice (called 'funk' at the time) which had in it the huge, complex outlook of imperialism, with its integral idea of manliness and also the almost irresistible pull of patriotism. In 1914, Britain and its empire was still, in spite of the debacle of the Anglo-Boer wars, a concept nourished and celebrated in thousands of publications offering boys' adventures. For grown-ups there were the male adventure genres, covering tales of derring-do in Africa and India, accounts of battles won by sheer pluck and daring; reminders of the sheer dogged heroism of Rorke's Drift back in 1879 in the war against the Zulu; and if defeats had to be mentioned, then the heroism involved was importantly foregrounded.

Add to this the importance of comradeship and brotherhood, and we have a strong, compelling assembly of reasons to hate and despise a coward. Much of this thought is in Sir Henry Newbolt's celebrated poem *Vitae Lampada*, in which the Colonel is dead, the Gatling gun is jammed and the voice of a schoolboy is heard shouting, 'Play up! Play up and play the game!' Ironically, a generation of soldiers before 1914 had experienced the 'game' of war in a shared leisure activity – the German-invented *Kriegspiel*, or 'war game'. In a report published in the *Journal of the Household Brigade for the Year 1871*, a Major Roerdanz had given a demonstration of this game at the United Services Institution, and the writer in the journal concludes, 'The War Office had taken the matter up, and the game was being introduced at all the principal military stations, but some delay must necessarily occur on account of the different formation of our Army.'

When the call to enlist came, as well as catering for the majority, it was also an opportunity for an ordinary to become special. The labourer and the grocer could suddenly be transformed into heroes; heads would turn when they walked into a room, and relatives would announce that their Bill or Joe had joined up and were going to fight the 'Boche'. They did indeed become special, and they had great courage, but the dissenting courage of the COs was never acknowledged.

The perceived action of cowardice, in this context, was seen as the lowest apathy and the most despicable evidence of a total lack of any moral compass. My own research showed evidence of just how long the shadow of shame extends in this respect. I had tried to arrange a meeting with a Welsh woman, after a chance meeting with her at a conference. She wanted to tell me about a CO in her family story. Then, the day before I was expecting to meet her, I was told that she didn't want to upset the family by helping to put the man's name into print. It was a matter of shame, even in 2014, a century on from the arrival of conscription.

Today, the historian has to find ways of moving closer to the attitudes behind this shame, and to the pro-war determination in 1914. It involves the challenge of understanding the past. Joseph Brodsky described this task very well: 'As failures go, attempting to recall the past is like trying to grasp the meaning of existence. Both make one feel like a baby clutching at a basketball; one's failures keep sliding off.' Nevertheless, one has to try, and there is a strong application of Brodsky's doubt when we consider the various pacifists and *refuseniks* of the First World War. This stems from a desperate and bold choice – something akin to daring to wear a white suit at a funeral. It is about a choice that goes against public opinion and stands out as perverse or morally wrong, but which is perhaps, more deeply, the kind of choice that raises a hand in a crowd of naysayers. It might well be bravery, but in 1914 – and more nakedly in 1916 – it was more prominently a denial of the will of the crowd.

Hence the stigma persists. Nothing changed when the next war came along. David Arscott relates a tale from oral history, coming from Ron Saunders, born in 1921:

> Refused call-up in the Second World War because of his work as a market gardener, he went to a village dance one evening and was chatting to a Canadian soldier when a girl presented him with a white feather in a Swan Vestas matchbox, the symbolic insult issued to non-combatants.
>
> 'Cor,' Ron says, 'He went very near willocky.'
>
> 'He went what?' I ask.
>
> 'Willocky ... He went wild, mairt.'

The shadow which still exists strangely prolongs the attitudes of what Elias Canetti called the 'baiting crowd':

> The baiting crowd forms with reference to a quickly attainable goal. The goal is known and clearly marked, and is also near ... The proclaiming of the goal, the spreading about of who it is that is to perish, is enough to make the crowd form. This concentration on killing is of a special kind and of an unsurpassed intensity. Everyone wants to participate ... Every arm is thrust out as if they all belonged to one.

BEFORE CONSCRIPTION: CLASH OF IDEOLOGIES

The Christian position regarding war is not clear. It shifts focus when the Old and New Testaments are compared. Some teachings allow for a 'just war' and some discount violence altogether. In the Sermon on the Mount, Jesus says, 'If anyone strikes you on the right cheek, turn to him the other also.' He also says, 'Love thine enemies and pray for those who persecute you.' Later, however, Christian thought allowed for Army service. Origen put forward the 'just war' theory, saying that a war could be fought under a 'legitimate ruler' to restore peace; this meant that war could therefore be seen as having an aim imbued with Christian love. As some apologists have argued, Moses, when he ordered the death of sinners, was in fact acting out of love.

The problem with the strict following of these precepts, as history has always shown, is that some authorities with secular power are hardly motivated by love of humanity. What can be easily discerned, however, is that the arrival of the First World War brought something new into this debate. Such was the scale of the conflict that both sides openly disobeyed Christian teachings, and also flouted rulings agreed at peace conferences.

However, one fundamental topic in Jesus' teachings stands as a foundation for the beliefs and actions of war resisters throughout history, and it was there in the minds of the men who said no to killing in 1914, and again after conscription was implemented in 1916. That is the notion that non-resistance, in the words of Herman Hoyt, leads to this: 'One of the first things a saved person is commanded to do is to separate himself from the practices of this world. Paul admonishes him to "be not conformed to this world". This covers all practices of life that make up the pattern of this present evil age.' Hoyt adds, 'A careful examination of Mathew 5:38–48 leads to the conclusion that physical violence is not Christian.'

Romain Rolland, the French novelist, saw the rift between those with power and those of faith immediately: 'The tragedy of our situation is that we are only a handful of free spirits – we are separated from the larger number of our army, from our people who are imprisoned and buried alive in the depth of the trenches. We should be able to speak to them but we cannot ... a dictatorial regime bears down on us all over Europe.'

This was the basis of the pacifist attitudes in the First World War. Simply, the COs, with their different faiths and ideologies, were nonconformists when it came to taking up arms against Germany. Of course, not all reasons for resistance were religious. As A. W. Zurbrugg has written, 'In Western Europe, the most vigorous opposition to militarism, going beyond the passing of anti-war resolutions, came from libertarians and syndicalists.' A number of left-wing thinkers saw that militarism tended to splinter and destroy industrial labour power, and it also often ruined the complete basis of the working-class solidarity that socialist movements had been steadily trying to create since the first struggles to make trade unions legitimate in the mid-nineteenth century. A large-scale war in Europe would override notions of brotherhood within the proletariat.

A brief historical survey of the background of this is needed before the main narrative begins.

*

In the century between the defeat of Napoleon at Waterloo in 1815 and the first reports of German atrocities in Belgium in 1914, Britain had steadily and relentlessly become a state with a total commitment to militarism and international expansion. This was driven by a paranoia based on the vulnerability of the North Sea as the German Baltic Fleet was enlarged. Strangely, at the same time that the Great Game of espionage was going on in the Far East with Russia, the huge British Empire was feeling vulnerable nearer to home. The result was a massive expansion of the volunteer regiments and the application of the Prussian system of having battalions of the regiments at home and abroad, on a cyclical basis. In plain terms, the result was a nation in a constant state of mental aggravation for war; exercises and manoeuvres abounded, and the Territorials could 'play soldiers' day and night. In the face of that, who could hear the voices calling out for peace and disarmament?

Welsh writers, social thinkers and preachers were part of that 'underground' voice for peace, like one plaintive voice in the midst of a great choral expression of warlike attitudes. As in all other areas of the United Kingdom, many COs were made in the midst of the war, rather than in the philosophies and beliefs in existence in 1914. Many were like the poet Gwenallt, who served in the

Army and later accepted and promulgated pacifism. A distinction existed between those who were sure of their conscience in 1914, and those who found that the war experience taught and changed them fundamentally. The voices who objected to war and refused to fight at the very beginning help us to understand today the feelings which were most pressing when conscription came about. A typical voice is that of Corder Catchpool, imprisoned for his beliefs, who wrote, 'Ah me! One can but do what one believes right and leave the rest. It would be infinitely easier to be out there again, whatever the dangers, than in prison, where, among other things, the human touch is gone.'

In January 1914, just five months before war with Germany was announced, *The Times* reported at length on a speech given by Lloyd George on armaments preparation by Germany; the report extended to several large paragraphs. Then, at the foot of the page, a small note was appended in contrast: the Peace Society had met and passed a motion that a statement in support of a peace declaration across Europe should be made and circulated. This was printed in a smaller typeface, something that would not be noticed by any grazing reader.

The whole idea of peace was seen then by the nationalists and imperialists as 'giving in'. Pacifism was defined widely as an inferior kind of thinking, as one newspaper report put it in November 1914, noting that factions in Germany were trying to use propaganda expressing a peace movement: 'They failed in that country [France] and the Germans may possibly transfer their attempt to this side of the Channel and try to work upon the softness of heart and brain among our own pacifists.'

Despite this, there was a robust lobby for pacifist sentiments and a determination to press for disarmament in British society, and

Welsh personalities were in the forefront of that campaign. Deep in the hearts of the Nonconformists across the chapels of Wales, there was a belief in humanitarian ideals, backed by the biblical injunction to 'love thy neighbour'. After all, the Bible was clear on this; the fundamental words from Luke 2:14 are, 'Glory to God in the highest, and on earth peace, good will toward men,' and along with Isaiah 52:7, 'How beautiful upon the mountains are the feet of him that bringeth good tidings, that publisheth peace'. This supported of the work of peacemakers; peacemakers, of course, 'are blessed'.

In particular, the Quaker faith was fundamental to the Peace Society's aims and existence. Love for fellow men and respect for human life lies at the centre of the tenets expressed by that group, and Christianity in general, of course, tells us to 'turn the other cheek'. In and even before 1914, there was an increasingly widespread awareness of the militarism of Germany, and such sentiments from the Bible could easily be interpreted as hopelessly naive in the face of a predominating realpolitik. Bismarck had unified the German states in 1870, and by the 1880s the German empire was expanding into Africa.

At the very base of the pro-war attitudes was the certain belief that the German navy, which had been the recipient of heavy and sustained investment for decades, was presenting the kind of threat that Britain had known before, from the Spanish Armada in 1588 and from Napoleon's build-up of flat boats for transporting troops across the Channel in 1803. Those with a long memory and an interest in British history could recount the fear expressed when Britain expected a massive French army to land at any moment in Essex and set about destroying 'civilisation'. Some would argue at the time that Wales and her coast had never known such tremors of imminent invasion, having only had the pathetic and raggle-taggle Fishguard invasion of 1797 in which, mythically, Jemima Nicholas and her lady-friends had repelled the invaders with pitchforks.

Yet the opposing line of thought was not worried by notions of soft-headedness or naivety. In the century since the end of the Napoleonic wars, advocates of peace had achieved quite a lot, culminating in the accomplishment of Sir William Randall Cremer, the radical who had created the Workmen's Peace Association in 1871, worked for inter-parliamentary union and had won the Nobel Peace Prize in 1903. He had even been bold enough to oppose the war in South Africa against the Boers in 1899.

The Peace Society at the time of the First World War had been in existence for almost a century, having been formed in 1816 after Waterloo to promote universal peace. It was largely a Welsh creation from the start, with Evan Rees as the first secretary; by 1848, Henry Richard of Tregaron was secretary. In 1915 another Welshman was to take charge: Herbert Dunnico. Peace was something worth a crusade, and in the nineteenth century it was attractive to a number of Welsh writers and thinkers. Of course, it was always going to struggle to make an imprint in the midst of so much clamour for imperial warmongering and expansion.

The Peace Society had been formed by Joseph Tregelles Price of Neath, a Quaker; from the middle of the century, Henry Richard, called 'the Apostle of Peace', took centre stage. He was the son of a Calvinist minister, educated at Llangeitho grammar school and subsequently in London, where he later became minister at the Marlborough Chapel. As secretary to the Peace Society, Richard was active in a much wider sphere, campaigning for international arbitration and notably present when the Treaty of Paris was conceived in 1856 – made in the aftermath of the Crimean War that had seen a loss of life on a large scale. He followed this by entering Parliament as a Liberal member for Merthyr in 1868, and then eleven years later he was made chairman of the Congregational Union of England and Wales.

Richard spoke and published prolifically on a number of causes, but pacifism was at the core of his aims and passionate advocacies. Unfortunately, after his death there was a gradual decline in its potency, and there has been criticism of its lack of teeth in the face of conscription in 1915. Herbert Dunnico, the Welshman who took over in 1915, at least tried to make the society's voice be heard. He even tried to call a truce with Germany in 1916, forming the Peace Negotiation Committee. Dunnico started work at a factory when he was a child, and rose through hard work and commitment to apply his socialist thinking in practical politics, becoming MP for Consett later in life. He was a Baptist as well as a left-wing thinker, and we have to have some sympathy for him in terms of 1914–16, when the media were controlled by the government and any voices of dissent were suppressed.

It is hard to exaggerate the achievement and influence of Henry Richard; he died in 1888 at Treborth, Bangor, valued and beloved for his writings on Wales generally, as well as for his work in promoting peace. What is undeniable is his lasting influence. In statements made by many of the new generation of COs, who confronted the tribunals to present their case against mass slaughter, we may see the lines of thought Henry Richard expressed, as in W. J. Chamberlain's account of the reasoning behind his refusal to take up arms; after running through the usual reasons for pacifism, he adds, in his book, *Fighting for Peace*, 'The essential vice of conscription is not that it necessitates the persecution of those who are determined not to yield to it, but that it breaks down the decent reluctance of the much greater number who have never thought of opposing the demands of constituted authority.'

This leads to a deeper level of understanding of the ideals which opposed the war attitude: the loss of individual liberty and moral choice. The pacifists realised that the nature of the Army was always one of total reliance on the hierarchical structure of command, a kind of obedience that negates personality and individual agency. By 1916 and the start of conscription this was made much more extreme, because by that time it was known that the English class system dictated Army rank; Sandhurst- and public school-trained officers treated their 'inferiors' like scum with neither sense nor dignity. Their concept of a 'man' went no further than a definition of the word equating with 'body'. Hence, military discipline, enforced by the provost officers, was one of physical punishment and deprivation, with the firing squad waiting for deserters and cowards.

*

Essentially, the attitude of total obedience, which depended on the sacrifice of individual lives for a greater good or ideal, had to keep on working through a mixture of fear and duty; the massive indoctrination machine of the newly expanded periodical presses of the 1890s and early Edwardian years made it clear that sacrifice for one's country was essential. Logically, this opened up the other, more complex dimension of the COs nature and stance, including the more profound and intractable elements of Liberalism. One of the great paradoxes of the will to destroy Germany and hate for German people in the years of the First World War is the cultural ties and interplay of ideas and art between Britain and Germany. The radical Liberals expected Lloyd George to take the lead in setting his thought against war, and so show that the philosophies underpinning his political party extended beyond mere topicality and ad hoc decisions, and included fundamental attitudes to mankind and society. He failed to meet these expectations, and consequently there were Welsh people of both dispositions – pro-German in cultural values and anti-German in all spheres.

Where does all this lead us in understanding the writers, thinkers, teachers and scholars, as well as the working men of principle on that fateful date of 4 August 1914? The fact is that their fate would follow a particular trajectory. First, an appearance at a tribunal, where they would face searching questions often loaded with prejudice; then they had to wait and see if their case would be considered as honest and rightful, or as a false claim resulting from cowardice or disobedience; finally the decision was made as to whether the man may be exempted from military service and continue life as a non-combatant, or if he would be condemned as a coward or traitor and imprisoned.

What really comes across from the life stories of those who suffered this experience is the confrontation between personal values, emotions such as shame and loss of face, and the misunderstanding and criticism of others; it might be said that while awaiting the outcome of such a tribunal, one had to rely on the spirit of Polonius's words in Hamlet in his advice to his son, Laertes:

> This above all: to thine own self be true,
> And it must follow, as the night the day
> Thou canst not then be false to any man.

This is a reminder that the hard part in such scenarios is keeping true to oneself, in a world in which to be different is a profound transgression. The contrary thought system of those in opposition to the CO of the time, and voiced by every private on leave, was that surely it was to the sergeant that one had to be true.

There was, of course, a socialist base from which a massive amount of literature was spawned. The general flavour of it was captured in Fred Bowers' words: 'Boys, don't do it ... Act the man! Act the brother! Act the human being! Property can be replaced – human life never. The idle rich class, who own and order you about, order us [politicians] about too. They and their friends own the land and the means of life in Britain.'

The nature and position of socialist thought and activity in relation to pacifism needs explaining before the focus moves to conscription. The emergence of pacifist lines of thought during the nineteenth century is not hard to explain. As the second phase of the Industrial Revolution arrived at the same time as working-class movements gained more status, the rights of the individual became more open to scrutiny, and these rights included the right to reject military service. The obvious need for greater harmony and cooperation between nations in order to facilitate trade in turn helped to create a sense of the brotherhood of workers. It became more apparent that the life and needs of the proletarian worker, selling his or her labour, were the same in Italy as in Russia, and in Germany as in Britain. In that frame of thinking, what purpose could a destructive war between nations possibly serve? The question was asked and answered in a number of places.

Since the achievement by the artisan class of the establishment of their union, the Amalgamated Society of Engineers, in 1851, there had been a call for a broader cultural sensibility on the part of the new arrivals in the middle class. This was the result of the gradual awakening of interest in European art and ideas, along with such leisure pursuits as travel and musical entertainment which followed, partly influenced by the writers of the Romantic movement who had sharpened awareness of other nations and non-British philosophy and politics. After all, throughout the nineteenth century Britain had been well aware of the growth of liberalism and of radical ideas in the ranks of the ordinary people. In fact, immigration from Eastern Europe and from Germany had served to broaden the knowledge and sense of empathy and curiosity in the British intellectuals. Of course, this was not enough to stop the bigoted persecution of Anglo-German communities and businesses at the start of the war, and particularly after the sinking of the *Lusitania* in 1915, but the recognition of some pan-European socialist ideas was there – it simply tended to be in advance of its time in terms of the numbers of people who were inclined to have an interest in such matters.

All this background is not to say that socialists before 1914 were also pacifists, but the theorists did have an understanding of the pacifist outlook, in terms of idealistic resolutions. Karl Marx's own words about raising the quality of life for working men by rejecting war between nations in favour of the far more important class war demonstrate this. A statement by the 1867 League of Peace and Freedom is far more informative, explaining that war 'weighs chiefly on the working class, in that it not only deprives it of the means of existence, but also constrains it to shed the workers' blood; armed peace paralyses the powers of production, demands of labour only useless tasks, and intimidates production.' The thinking that was fundamental to socialism included the notion that first there necessarily has to be a new order of society, and then a chance that peace will follow.

In the 1907 congress of the Second International, a climate of international tension led socialists to adopt a different position regarding war. Some agreed that socialists should be in favour of a war that was 'just' – a struggle that would liberate workers or slaves. Others argued that socialism should be in favour of the idea that socialists should join in a conflict, if only to create an insurrection in their ranks and attain the revolution which would make the new order of things. This was a chaotic debate, but the congress tried to make a statement which all would accede to. The result was a statement containing these words:

> If a war threatens to break out, it is the duty of the working class and of its parliamentary representatives in the country involved, supported by the consolidating activity of the International Socialist Bureau, to exert every effort to prevent the outbreak of war by means they consider most effective, which naturally vary according to the accentuation of the class struggle and of the general political situation ...

The problem for the COs later, when war arrived, was evident in the attitudes to pacifism among the workers and their organisations generally. At the 1913 Trades Union Congress meeting, for instance, as a mere footnote to the report on business conducted, we have this: 'Resolutions were adopted against conscription and in favour of the peace movement and in support of reform in legal administration.' This smacks of a simple, almost perfunctory statement which has no real importance. In fact, the lukewarm attitudes to peace activism were evident in the volte-face in the actions of many lovers of socialist theory who, when war came, chose to support the government.

Fenner Brockway, one of the originators of the NCF, described the conflicting attitudes towards pacifism, first in terms of great optimism, as he felt that there was an emerging pan-European solidarity of socialist pacifism:

> In the *Labour Leader* ... I committed the ILP to opposition to the war. I did so without the opportunity of consultation, but I had no doubt what the Party attitude would be; all were anti-militarist, anti-war. We ran a slogan across the top of the paper: 'German socialists are our Comrades still' and the front page was devoted to a black-type manifesto denouncing the war as imperialist. The following Sunday, the National Council of the ILP met in a dismal pub by the Irwell. The members were overwhelmingly against the war, only two dissenting.

Brockway then added, referring to Keir Hardie (the ILP leader), that he was depressed by a sense of failure, having been unable to exert influence at the Socialist International congress and 'now the same socialist leaders, with a few brave exceptions, were supporting their governments'. It destroyed Hardie's faith and hope.

*

Immediately before August 1914 there had been a long debate on conscription in the press. An authority on military matters, William Jesser Coope, wrote a substantial essay for *The Times* in which he argued strongly for a complete revision of military training and for national service. His opinion of conscription was a common one: 'It is hardly reasonable to expect that Englishmen will accept conscription as readily as the men of continental nations, who cannot fail to understand that they have land frontiers to defend and cannot be unaware that in the last century their countries have been invaded.' His conclusion was that the state should 'secure what we have not got at present – a highly-trained army of picked men'. In December 1913, Lord Roberts, who was president of the National Service League, felt that he had to set the record straight with regard to exactly what the aims of his organisation were. He wrote that there was no question of conscription after the continental method being adopted in Britain, and added, 'We earnestly ask that the great national question of the adoption of compulsory national service for home defence may be considered ... The freedom and independence of our country and the liberty to work out our own salvation in our own way ... are matters of vital importance to every British citizen.'

We have here the paradox that, seven months before Kitchener was to call for his new army, the notion of home defence conscription was a hot topic, and was feared as a threat to individual liberty. Added to this was the Unionist threat over in Ireland, in which Sir Edward Carson was threatening a war to keep the North of Ireland out of any political change. This prompted a response, expressed well by Arthur Betts, who argued that conscription would bring into the Army 'a rising generation ... combating the class evil which is prevalent among the fighting men'.

Of course, when the appeals came for new Army recruits, many enlisted as free men; the panoply of national feeling and traditions of heroic idealism became evident across the land and were frequently the reason cited for joining up. It is interesting to note that the media instilled idealised visions of the England that the volunteer army were enlisting to save. In 1926, while gathering material for his book *In Search of England*, H. V. Morton had this experience:

> A little London factory hand whom I met during the war confessed to me, when pressed, and after great mental difficulty, that he visualized the England he was fighting for – the England of the 'England wants you' poster – as not London, not his own street, but as Epping Forest, the green place where he had spent Bank Holidays. And I think most of us did … The village and the English countryside are the germs of all we are.

There was also an attraction to the 'glamour' of enlisting. One way to understand this is explained by the photographic work of Christina Broom, the suffragette who also ran a photography postcard business; Lucy Davies wrote, with Broom in mind, 'Her portraits were purchased in their hundreds by soldiers who sent them home to their families; she did more for conscription, Field Marshall Frederick Roberts said, than his prayers for new recruits ever had.'

Who still thought of 'individual liberty' when the war fever took hold? Only a minority, and those people are the subjects of the following chapters.

2

THE NO-CONSCRIPTION FELLOWSHIP

As the war began, the government wasted no time in stepping up national security. There was a sense of spy mania in the air, and on 8 August the Defence of the Realm Act was passed. The nation had been at war only four days when John Maclean, a socialist and anti-war campaigner from Clydeside, was arrested 'for uttering statements deemed prejudicial to recruiting'. He was fined, sent to prison and sacked from his teaching job. The paranoia and repression had begun. DORA was conceived in order to give the government a whole raft of emergency powers which would be necessary, it was argued, in the war effort. In fact, it was legislation that was to prove nastily effective against COs, as its authoritarian measures took hold. Censorship was at the core of the rulings, expressed most cogently in these words: 'No person shall by word of mouth or in writing spread reports likely to cause disaffection or alarm among any of His Majesty's forces or among civilian population.'

To understand where this came from, an account of the paranoia associated with spy mania is needed. This links to the background of German and British military intelligence advances in the pre-war years.

In 1917 the writer D. H. Lawrence was staying in Zennor, Cornwall, with his German wife, Frieda. They stayed for a time at the Tinner's Arms and then rented a house, Higher Tregerthen. There was a good deal of suspicion from the locals. Here were a couple, staying by the sea on an isolated stretch of coastline, and the woman was a German. Rumours began to circulate that the couple were signalling to German submarines. Stories abounded, including rumours that there were smoke signals from their chimney or that there was a supply of petrol for the submarines below the adjacent cliffs; people thought they heard German songs being sung in the house. After all, they reasoned, the route for the Atlantic convoys was close by. The couple were stopped and searched as they carried shopping home. They were not the only temporary residents in the area, and others, like Lawrence, had been rejected for conscription or had somehow avoided it.

In his letters Lawrence wrote that he was as 'innocent even of pacifist activities, let alone spying of any sort, as the rabbits of the field outside'. It all led to a military exclusion order and they had to leave. Had the locals known that Frieda was actually Frieda von Richthofen, a relative of the Red Baron fighter pilot, there may well have been even more trouble. This episode in Lawrence's tempestuous life was a template example of the spy fever that swept the country before and during the First World War. Perhaps the most typical example of this irrational paranoia was the accusation that Frieda was signalling by using clothes on her washing line. The mass media were largely to blame for this, and they built on the fears already in existence in literature. As far back as 1871, Colonel G. T. Chesney had written *The Battle of*

Dorking, in which there is an imagined Franco-Russian invasion of England. The novel created all kinds of spin-off stories, and sales were huge – 80,000 copies sold. Then, in 1906, William Le Queux published *The Invasion of 1910*. This was something new: an account of an invasion supposedly just a few years in the future, and the attackers were the Germans, a nation with a new empire vying with England for national supremacy.

A play called *An Englishman's Home* ran for over a year and was filmed in 1914. The enemy, though not referred to as Germans, wore spiked helmets and so the reference was obvious. Early spy films involved the Royal Navy, partly due to the furore over the building (or shelving) of dreadnoughts.

Le Queux is a particularly interesting figure because he became involved in espionage, albeit in an amateur way. He was often just a propagator of myths, but he made a number of effective statements on the potential threat from Europe to Britain's domestic security. He claimed to have contacts in Berlin and that he had furthermore been supplied with a list of British traitors there. He wrote that there was a secret group in Germany called the Hidden Hand, and although he had no proof he insisted that the traitors on the list included very prominent people in Britain, including politicians and writers. He even managed to team up with the distinguished soldier, Lord Roberts, to organise a make-believe invasion – an action which had serious repercussions. With the help of the *Daily Mail* they turned the affair into a fiasco that generated national fears regarding the vulnerability of English shores and defences against attack and invasion. It was a classic example of the journalistic stratagem of creating a terrifying 'might be' situation in order to make the government act, as in recent times when a journalist might board a train with a mysterious parcel and not be stopped and searched by anyone.

Le Queux's romantic and playful world of spying was the sort of activity at home in England that provoked fear and suspicion among civilians, such as imagining hidden German arsenals and spies in disguise as ordinary workmen. What is sure is that his warnings and fabrications caught the attention of Colonel James Edward Edmonds, and via him, the Committee for Imperial Defence.

There were certainly German agents in England; they were here to buy information, make sketches from observation, write reports, study communication systems and, in particular, to ascertain the true nature of British naval power. Naturally, there were spies in the field as well, and the propaganda machine made it clear what was happening to them. A typical story, printed in the popular press, was that of a tale told by an American Ambulance Field Service volunteer:

> Early one morning a soldier appeared in a trench. He started chatting with some passing poilus [soldiers in the French infantry]. He told them he was inspecting the lines and they showed him around their trenches ... He wandered around the woods with his new-found friends, who showed him the positions of many guns. As night came on, he ... left his friends and went to the trenches. He told the sentry he had orders to inspect the barbed wire ... The man never returned ... there is little doubt that he was a German spy.

Magazines such as *The British Magazine* showed graphic photographs of German spies being executed by firing squads or dead and tied to stakes by the roadside.

In 1911, before the outbreak of the war, Kell's arrest of the hairdresser Karl Ernst was the start of a remarkable operation against spies, and this generated the mania that followed. Reports of Ernst's spy network were everywhere and were subject to great exaggeration. These stories came to editors in fragments and with a sense of high drama – men seen messing with telephone cables in Dover or the Officer Training Corps at Berkhamsted being called out to block the road as a German armoured car advanced on London. Some views on these stories are that they were intentional, the work of the intelligence men. After all, this was the time when intelligence work was taking up the Wolseley notions of ruses, tricks and deceptions. The expert writer on these matters was Arthur Ponsonby, whose book of 1928, *Falsehood in War*, summarised the deliberate lies which circulated during the First World War. Some of these stories were mentioned by a reviewer at the time:

> They include many atrocity stories, such as that of the nurse with her breast cut off; the Belgian baby without hands; the crucified Canadian soldier – and most famous of all, the corpse factory in which the Germans were said to process their dead in order to extract from them materials for munitions.

However, the fact remains that there was indeed a network of German spies, and solid research by Thomas Boghardt has increased our understanding of how this worked, and indeed how it was stopped. Boghardt has shown that the Admiralstab in Germany were not very successful in accessing and using the large number of Germans already living in Britain at the time. In 1911 there were 56,000 such people, but not many of them were sympathetic to the *Kaiserreich*. Widenmann, the naval attaché in London, pointed out that a large percentage of these people were acculturated English, many of whom had integrated into industrial communities (as in Bradford, for instance, a city with a long-established German population).

The German intelligence network therefore had to look elsewhere for recruits. As Boghardt notes, the foremost spies in the ring – Schultz, Grosse, Graves and Hentschel – were actually criminals: Grosse was in prison at the time he was brought into espionage work. A summary of what Max Schultz did and what obstacles he encountered will illustrate the nature of the challenge for Germany at the time. In basic terms, he was a disaster. He was taken out of an asylum in order to spy – a fact that demonstrates Germany's desperation. Parties were regular affairs on his houseboat, and while high at one such party he accidentally shot his housekeeper. He was notably unhinged in most respects, and after trying to suborn a solicitor to the cause of espionage he was watched by the police day and night. This all happened in Plymouth, where he was sent in 1911.

The network was controlled by 'N' – the code name for the *Admiralstab* director, Arthur Tapken – and he must have been bitterly disappointed in this particular agent. Kell and his team were never particularly worried about Shultz; eventually he was tried, but received only a short sentence before he left England.

This pre-war espionage operation was based on an initially confused notion on the part of the *Admiralstab* about which navy would be the biggest threat in the immediate future; apart from Britain, France and Russia were also potential enemies. However, once things became settled and Grand Admiral Tirpitz took over as Secretary of State of the German Imperial Naval Office, the focus turned to London and the major British ports. As there was no clear line of thought with the aim of making the Royal Navy its potential target, there was always a certain amount of blurred thinking behind the espionage measures. The first plan was simple, to use the German naval attaché in London as the underpinning communication channel, and to have men planted in most major ports, with all systems communicating via telegram. However, there were several flaws to this plan, chief among them that if ever the attaché had to be elsewhere nothing could be done from the ports – even if that absence coincided with something of great military importance.

The attaché was Widenmann, and he was both reluctant and somewhat dilatory. When the *Admiralstab* tried to set communication in motion, there were usually excuses as to why their attempts failed. Eventually, the controller gave in and decided to work with individual civilians, and there lies the heart of the following failure. Arguably, the most successful agent was Gustav Steinhauer, a man who certainly felt pride in his achievements, later writing his memoirs under the title *The Kaiser's Master Spy: The Story as Told by Himself* (1930).

*

Central to the paranoia about spies was the ever-growing possibility of invasion. The reasons behind this are principally related to the German navy. It is important to grasp the fact that the concept of a navy was very new in Germany. Since Bismarck's unification of the German states in 1870, there had been a long and difficult fight by notable individuals to establish a navy that would be confident in confronting Britain's Royal Navy. In the latter half of the nineteenth century, the tiny German fleet was actually trained and supplied by Britain, though on a very small scale. It was a case of Britain – with its massive fleet spread throughout its Empire – looking upon Germany as a minuscule, almost childlike operation.

The Prussian military mindset was always fixed on land armies. Prussia and its new accretions from other states in the newly unified German nation were of the fixed opinion that it could easily defeat Britain on land. The older statesmen – including the aging Bismarck, who was in his eighties when Tirpitz started his campaign for a proper navy – would have to be persuaded. Tirpitz, a great admirer of the Royal Navy and of most aspects of English life and culture, actually visited Bismarck and talked him into backing his plan to build more battleships.

The entrenched attitudes towards sea power in Germany were focused on the notion of using cruisers and, later, torpedo boats, instead of investing huge amounts of money in a fleet of battleships. Most military men thought that it would be pointless to try and take on Britain with battleships – they preferred the idea of attacking the British fleets with faster and more manoeuvrable ships. Tirpitz, on the other hand, was convinced that a battleship fleet was essential to security, particularly as the German empire grew and the threat from France and Russia declined. At a review in 1897, when the Royal Navy displayed 165 warships extending over 30 miles, it was the cause of a certain amount of consternation among the German high command who were resisting Tirpitz. When he pushed his Navy Bill and talked the Kaiser into supporting him, it was the beginning of a success in his struggle for a German navy.

Tirpitz had his Navy Bill ratified in 1898: thirty-eight battleships were to be built over a planned programme of seventeen years. It was partly the admiral's 'risk theory' which had won the day. This had suggested that a huge empire such as Britain's would require large emplacements of the Royal Navy across the world, and would therefore never have a force on the domestic front too large for the German navy to tackle should there ever be an attack on the German harbours. Another option in strategic thinking about defence was that of creating two chief ports – one in the Baltic and one on the North Sea – creating a two-tier obstacle for any fleet launching an aggressive attack on Germany. All this explains the growing fear of a German presence in the North Sea, which had never been there previously.

But there was also something else urging for German espionage in Britain to be taken seriously: there had been a major scare before, and not so long ago, in 1882. In that year, the fear was one of a French assault, and by means of a Channel tunnel. For decades, the notion of 'splendid isolation' had been a basic belief of the imperialists. But with the possibility of a tunnel across that critically significant 21 miles of the Atlantic, apprehensions grew. The Channel Tunnel Company had been formed after a plan conceived in parliament and a bill put in process; its offices in London soon came under siege. There was a widespread opposition to the idea of a tunnel, with a petition signed by such celebrities as Lord Tennyson and Cardinal Newman. Naturally, in the popular press there was a conception of a spy – a French spy, usually disguised as a waiter. When the opposition was joined by the great Sir Garnet Wolseley, there was a profound bolstering of the cause's credibility. He expressed the view that a few thousand armed men, travelling through the tunnel in disguise, could easily become a platform for a seriously destabilising invasion of England.

Regarding the possibility of a German invasion, one of the most influential factors from the world of literature was Erskine

Childers' novel, *The Riddle of the Sands* (1903), published just two years after Kipling's *Kim*. The contrast is significant: Kim treats the Great Game in a manner exactly in keeping with that phrase – it is a narrative of spy-craft entirely concerned with the element of intelligence tied to battle and empire, and conducted in a world of gentlemen-officers. Childers, by contrast, gives his readers an image of espionage linked to the inexorable advance of a rapidly industrialising civilisation next door to Britain. The two main characters sailing in the North Sea come across fictional examples of Tirpitz's fleet: referring to Germany, Childers' character Davies says, 'We aren't ready for her; we don't look her way. We have no naval base in the North Sea and no North Sea fleet ...'

A strong presence in Childers' novel, then, is the theme of England's complacency. The references to the rather tired and effete nation that was once young, aggressive and thrusting forward in conquest is present in the novel as a dispiriting comparison to the contemporary British Empire. The fears about the protection of the homeland are always there – entirely in keeping with a world in which the Navy League and the societies of riflemen flourished. The militaristic culture of Britain at the time, from the boys' brigades to the regiments of volunteers, is easily understood as a reaction to those fears Childers describes.

Summing up the spy mania of the Edwardian years, it has to be said that our understanding is influenced in large part by the nature of the wars Britain fought throughout the nineteenth century. They were distant ones. That simple fact explains so much, as the very idea of an enemy on the doorstep was terrifying in contrast to the previous concept of war – one in which regiments were seen off from the quayside at Portsmouth on their way to the Crimea, South Africa or India. It had been the case for a very long time that one war followed another and the movements of troops had happened to meet particular emergencies. Most were small-scale combats involving the normal groupings of imperial infantry, artillery and various deployments of cavalry. Intelligence had always been integral to those movements, either included with artillery or left to the control of the Adjutant General. Slowly, ever since 1873, intelligence work had become something to be understood and undertaken separately, with its own specialisms and responsibilities. The Fenian bombings at the very heart of the Empire had shown that something new was needed, something as ruthless and efficient as the potential enemies could be.

It has to be said that the spy network was indeed beaten because of hard work. In fact, it cannot be denied that the methods of the comparatively new CID men were at the heart of the success. Police work against anarchists and communists was notably successful, as in one typical account of Special Branch men from 1909 involving two robbers who were Latvian immigrants. The men, Hefeld and Lepidus, were armed when they robbed a rubber factory in Tottenham High Road; there was a police station opposite the scene of the crime. The robbers waited for a car to arrive in which two men were carrying the wages of the company's workers. A pursuit followed, including a gunfight, and the two fugitives were so desperate that one shot himself in the head rather than be taken; the other did the same later while under siege. Detectives were collaborating with Metropolitan police forces against gangs of anarchists, with the chase involving both branches. In other words, normal detective practice in civilian matters was there for Kell to learn from. Liaison between different parts of the country was well established by that time; in fact, decades before, in a famous case in which several detectives were corrupted by a forgery gang, regional undercover work had tracked down the culprits, and also a concerted interception of mail had been undertaken. Kell was learning from the experts.

By 1909 when Kell needed such help, the detective branch had become skilled in such basic strategies as disguise, using informers, infiltration and some basic forensic science such as fingerprinting. They had also learned how to work with other organisations and how to utilise local knowledge. All this would become vital in the work against German spies in the ports. The spy Olsson, in Grimsby, for instance, was noticed and then 'tapped' – he must have been tailed and traced with a high degree of sophistication. The port of Grimsby was accustomed to a military presence at that time for other reasons, mainly a major strike and confrontation in 1903 in which a very heavy police and Army presence was required. Some of Kell's other 'clients' had been to that port as a matter of course. Common sense would have told MI5 that the Humber Estuary, with both Hull and Grimsby as prime targets, was the logical place for members of a spy network to be placed – Childers territory.

In the end, the German espionage ring was beaten by traditional solid police work, but Kell had a dash of genius. What he must have been surprised by, however, was the element of novelty and enterprise shown by the enemy too, as the intelligence team had to cope with different initiatives as the war came on. Tammy Proctor, for example, has shown that there was a female presence in espionage at the time, though only small-scale. Colonel Edmonds had something to say on this matter: 'The use of women in procuring intelligence for Germany is very considerable, and extends from ladies down to professional *horizontales* ...' Proctor makes it clear that most of the women detained for espionage were not born in England and many were interned without a trial. A large number of these were deported at the end of the war; British women who might be suspected were usually simply trailed and monitored or even sent to a convent as a substitute for prison. Again, interception of mail was the usual method of tracking these women down.

Throughout the whole course of the First World War, only thirty people were formally charged with spying, but beyond this there was a massive number of individuals who had been blacklisted; on the MI5 lists there was an astoundingly high number of some 27,000 files and many more individuals monitored, ranging from observations and blacklisting for ideological unsoundness to mere intellectual expression of such things as pro-German feelings, writings or social-cultural pursuits. It has to be recalled that in the course of the war on the home front there had been savage riots, such as the violence in Liverpool after the sinking of the *Lusitania* in 1915, and the disorder in Deptford in which 15,000 people roamed around the streets looking for German shops and restaurants to destroy. In the latter case, it took hundreds of police and men from the Army Service Corps to bring the trouble to an end.

Spy mania, then, in terms of its widespread media-generated myths and legends, played a part in the perceptions of Kell's work and indeed of the work done by all the professions involved in national security. But it also highlighted the depth of social paranoia beneath the peacetime patina of home security and middle-class progress. The new age of the proliferation of city commuters and the suburbs was also the age of amateur militarism and of insecurity. One thinks of those thousands of people holidaying in Skegness ('so bracing') who must have been looking out to sea, imagining a fleet of German warships across that tranquil water.

Writing in 1956, Douglas Browne assessed the liaison at the time of the First World War between Special Branch and intelligence:

The value of the work of Special Branch in connection with espionage caused it, toward the end of the war, to be so closely associated with Military Intelligence that it was virtually seconded from the CID; and in 1919 the experiment was tried of detaching it altogether. It became a separate department under an Assistant Commissioner who was styled Director of Intelligence.

*

In this setting, in which the British government expected espionage to function as part of a wider attack or even invasion from Germany, the first and central organisation of the COs, the No-Conscription Fellowship, was born. Within a few months of war beginning, the German Zeppelin airships had attacked some East Coast towns, and later London itself. Consequently, anyone disseminating unacceptable views about war and campaigning against recruitment was perceived as acting in a manner tantamount to aiding the enemy.

The NCF was also born in this political climate. In 1919, Fenner Brockway, writing with the experience of a prison sentence behind him, recounted the origins of the NCF. He wrote that in late 1914, when he was editing the *Labour Leader*, he appealed for the names of those who would not render military service. He further wrote that the response was so immediate that he saw the need for an official group – a fellowship – of like-minded objectors, or 'resisters' as he termed them.

In November 1914 the organisation was formed with over three hundred members, and a committee was created. The leading figures were Brockway himself, Clifford Allen (the chairman) and C. H. Norman. The Brockways' cottage in Derbyshire was, at first, the centre of administration, and by early 1915, the membership had expanded considerably. It didn't take long for the threat of conscription to become real. In 1914, in the first eager flush of enlistment in response to the campaign of Lord Kitchener for his new army – to be called the Pals' battalions – there had been no problem in furnishing the theatre of war; but by mid-1915, with the huge numbers of infantry needed in the stalemate of trench warfare which had emerged after the first battles, and with deaths and casualties so alarmingly high, a different approach to recruitment was needed. In August 1915, in what became known as Lord Derby's Scheme, compulsory enlistment began, initially with a process of 'attestation' in which men between eighteen and forty-one who were unmarried signed a form to state that they would answer the call to join the ranks when needed. Brockway wrote, 'The Derby Recruiting Campaign was then in full swing and everyone realised that the testing time approached. The most detailed plans were made to face every emergency. The whole organisation, from the branches to the National Committee, was built in duplicate, in case the authorities might attempt to suppress it.'

Clifford Allen also gave an account of the very heart of the NCF, which states the basis of the COs attitudes and resolutions:

The No-Conscription Fellowship is an organisation of men likely to be called upon to undertake military service in the event of conscription, who will refuse from conscientious motives to bear arms, because they consider human life to be sacred, and cannot, therefore, assume the responsibility of inflicting death. They deny the right of governments to say, 'You shall bear arms' and will oppose every effort to introduce compulsory military service into Great Britain. Should such efforts be successful, they will, whatever the consequences may be, obey their conscientious convictions rather than the commands of governments.

The COs were a mixed lot, holding their convictions from a wide basis of standpoints of faith and/or belief. The majority held a moral objection to war. This was founded on a fundamental belief about the nature of the relationships between human beings across the world; some, as Allen noted, had read Tolstoy, or were socialists of various hues. But whatever their stance, the moral objectors accepted the basic tenet of a brotherhood of man.

Another group were the political objectors, who saw conscription, as Allen put it, as 'a fatal infringement of human liberty ... because they feared that industrial freedom would be menaced by military compulsion'. Many in this category also looked back into recent history and argued that British foreign policy was mostly to blame for the advent of war, and that capitalism, over-riding human values, had been maintained by the corrupt who were in power.

There were also, of course, the religious resisters; it was against Christian teaching to take another life. In a powerful essay by Dr Alfred Salter, 'The Religion of a CO', which was printed in massive numbers, with over one and a half million copies being distributed across Britain, that religious position is explained and defended with eloquence and authority. Salter wrote that all mankind splits into two religions – the materialistic and the spiritual. The latter values all human life and teaches reverence and respect for others, whereas the former believes that 'Force alone matters' and adds, 'that is the gospel of materialism, which for the time being, seems to be the accepted doctrine of Europe, and the doctrine which is being preached from nearly every pulpit in England.' Salter concluded that, 'You will only conquer brutality by kindness. You will only supersede militarism by developing in the hearts of all peoples the spirit of brotherhood and forbearance.'

The Quaker element was strong, but it has to be made clear here that not all Quakers acted to object to the war in complete, fundamental terms. As Harvey Gillman has written, 'The First World War saw large Quaker meetings in a number of prisons, when many of them refused to have anything to do with fighting whatsoever ... One or two Quakers did enlist, believing it was a just war.' (The explanation for this is that in the ranks of Quakers there are absolutists and relativists, with the latter merely attempting to lessen the effects and miseries of a war, rather than refusing to participate in any way in the conflict.)

Fundamentally, these first COs in the new and bold NCF were trying to take a view of a pressing war from a distant stance, one involving philosophical scepticism and a degree of idealism and individualism that aimed to defy the often thoughtless obedience to act when the state calls on notions of public service and duty. G. K. Chesterton understood this objective view, and in an essay called 'The Conscript and the Crisis', written in 1912 when wars in various corners of Europe were in the air and discussed at dinner, he takes the theme that 'very few of us ever see the history of our own time happening'. He describes a stroll in a French town and his seeing a scene in the cathedral in which there was a special service being held for the conscripts. He wrote, 'There are many reasons for becoming a soldier. It may be a matter of hereditary luck or abject hunger or heroic virtue ... it may be an interest in the work ... but there are always two or three kinds of people who would never tend to soldiering; all those kinds of people were there.' He understood something fundamental to wars and their place in the ordinary lives of the citizenry of states. He saw that at the core of forced recruitment there is a certain callousness, an exploitation of the weak. He then adds to that the place of the Church; and although he does not openly criticise it, his remarks foreshadow the work of the padres at the front in the First World War, playing their part in the ideology of sacrifice: 'The priest ... said that war was hateful, and that we all hated it but that in all things reasonable the law of one's own commonwealth was the voice of God.'

It was this kind of insight, seeing human beings caught within the massive, heartless militaristic machine of their time, which led to the establishment of the NCF.

As a celebratory booklet published by the NCF in 1919 makes clear, the members were proud of their achievement, and their explanations make a stirring account of what was a vexed meeting of an idealistic philosophy of life with a war-fashioned world of sheer pragmatism. The booklet was written in a climate of heated political debate, social division and a great deal of anger, as various radicals came forward with criticisms of the handling of the post-war return to supposed normality, and the socialist activists and general protesters spoke, published and discussed openly a whole range of difficult issues. For instance, Ernest Thurtle's tract, *Shootings at Dawn*, went to press, and his anger must have excoriated all those readers who had hastened the call to arms. These were tales of men who had been shot by firing squad for cowardice – and there had been no sympathy for any factors of mental illness that might have been implied in their condition. Thurtle wrote, 'The names of the unfortunate victims have been deliberately suppressed, in order to avoid the possibility of giving unnecessary pain to relatives or friends, though letters I have received from some relatives indicate that they, having suffered cruel bereavement from the operation of this harsh law, are prepared for any kind of publicity which will help to get the law abolished.'

The booklet, *The No-Conscription Fellowship: A Souvenir of its work during the years 1914–1919*, informed the general public of dozens of issues and experiences that most of them had probably never considered before.

This memento begins with a summary of the important statistics: 6,312 people arrested for resisting the Military Service Acts; 5,970 COs court-martialled; 816 COs served prison sentences of over two years; 69 COs died after arrest, and 39 COs were mentally deranged. The casualties were high, but no one outside the organisation was ever interested in the facts and figures. The lists of the fallen of course, took all the attention.

The treasurer of the NCF, Edward Grubb, wrote with a sense of the wider issues at stake 'War has not ended war; Satan has not cast out Satan. The world is still bleeding and starving; it is yet in the grip of the forces that divide nation from nation, class from class and man from man.' In the retrospective of 1919, the organisation was proud of its achievements, and its administration had proved worthy of trust. Three main associations had hence branched out from the founding organisation – these were the Friends Service Committee, the Fellowship of Reconciliation and the NCF. They worked closely together, with a coordinating body known as the Joint Advisory Council (JAC). Dr Henry Hodgkin was Chairman of the Fellowship of Reconciliation.

There was a need, in this special publication, to have a typical witness account by a man whose experience could accurately represent the common suffering and also the shared credo. The man in question was Bernard Douglas Taylor, and he was just nineteen years old when arrested. He was a Manchester cabinet-maker, and he found that his refusal to fight took him to France enforced as a soldier, the state refusing to accept neither his plea nor his statement. He expressed his situation thus:

> For the past five months I have been attached to the Army I have obeyed no orders and received no pay. All three tribunals have recognised my convictions, but have failed to grant me the absolute exemption which the Military Service Act provides ... Therefore I stand here as a civilian and not as a soldier. When I refused to obey the order given I stated that I was a conscientious objector.

The most momentous occasion for the NCF was at the Memorial Hall in London on 27 November 1915, and Clifford Allen's speech contained the best case for their existence: 'We discovered a fact, which is the most important characteristic of our organisation, that there was one objection to conscription which we all shared with intense fervour, and that was a belief in the sanctity of human life.'

There were some open-minded responses to the NCF and its first real assertion of presence. J. H. Thomas, MP, wrote a letter to Allen which was then printed in *The Times*:

> It is amazing to me how some people glibly talk of conscription as if it only had to be introduced to be accepted as a necessary blessing in this war. I have disagreed – and disagree today – with your attitude on the war, but I feel bound to say, as one anxious for the cause of

the Allies, that I know of nothing so calculated to divide the nation, so likely to embarrass the government and so certain to be resented by the workers, as conscription.

Few could have done such welcome, media-friendly work for the NCF. But there soon came repression, and it showed in a variety of events. For instance, on 29 May 1916, Frederick Halfpenny, a clerk for the London County Council, was charged with making 'circular statements likely to cause disaffection or to prejudice recruiting and discipline'. He was secretary of the Forest Gate branch of the NCF. His counsel argued that Halfpenny did not order the sending out of an offending paragraph which read as follows:

> When in custody, members must be guided by their own judgement ... but they should decline to sign documents, accept Army pay, undergo drill, or put on regimentals ... They should be cheerful, courteous and friendly in all circumstances. Members should ask for the right to consult their friends with any sentence passed by court-martial.

Halfpenny was fined £50, with 90 days in prison as the alternative. That was a very large fine – the equivalent of around £2,000 today.

After the circulation of the leaflets protesting the imposition of conscription, many of the leaders of the NCF had large fines imposed. Six of them, on 17 May, were found guilty under the same DORA offences, and fined £100 and £10 costs. Sir Alfred Newton insisted that the leaflet would 'prejudice recruiting and the discipline of the Army'.

The first Military Service Act had stirred the COs into action.

*

Mention must also be made of the Union of Democratic Control, whose members made it clear that, in the words of one of their detractors, 'if democracy, or any other form of government requires universal military service, they will refuse to render it.' This was not a pacifist group, though its concerns bordered on some of the oppositional stances taken against the war. It was created in 1914 with a primary purpose of establishing reforms in foreign policy, and was founded by Charles Trevelyan and Ramsay MacDonald. Left-wing thinkers and politicians in both the Labour and Liberal parties lent their support, including Arnold Rowntree, Norman Angell and Philip Morrell, along with Labour leaders such as H. N. Brailsford and Philip Snowden. The group wanted a revision of war aims, and a more effective scrutiny of the reasons for the conflict. There were over a hundred local branches by 1917, but in contrast with the NCF its activities appear to have been more concerned with speeches, theories and Fabian tactics than by direct action and confrontation.

However, in early 1916, there was the matter of the new legislation, like a great edifice in need of being moved. The NCF took the lead, and it was going to be a long and bitter struggle.

Attention must now turn to that Military Service Act.

3

THE MILITARY SERVICE ACT AND THE TRIBUNALS

At first, during the public debate on the imminent war in early August 1914, those who argued for conscription did so with only home defence in their thoughts. The growth of the German navy and the advent of the Zeppelins lay behind this position of necessary action. As Michael and Eleanor Brock point out, Lord Northcliffe, who was a powerful voice in the formation of opinion, 'was opposed to sending a single British soldier to the Continent'. In that atmosphere, when the talk was all of the German atrocities against 'Little Belgium', as the Brocks add further, conscription was almost a dirty word. 'Conscription was the touchstone. In the changed mood the impression grew that the cabinet were refusing to prepare for it, not because it would be impractical, but because their whole past made them revolt against this kind of compulsion.' How different things were to be two years later. But in the meantime, men rushed to join up.

The initial massive recruitment of 1914 and the creation of the Pals' battalions had happened on the crest of a wave of enthusiasm for the war; Germany would have to pay for the moral outrage of what had been perpetrated on Belgium and France, and also for the unspeakable effrontery of bombing English towns. That militarisation had occurred within a context of a hatred of conscription; the operative notion being that going to war was assuredly something that a free-born Brit did willingly, for moral reasons. The enthusiasm was sustained throughout the end of 1914 and into the first four months or so of 1915, but then came the mass deaths of the battles resulting from the need to keep Ypres and the coastal towns, entailing huge losses in the ranks of the professional soldiers.

When the new men of Kitchener's army finally arrived in France and faced battle for the first time, the shock of such high casualty rates began to hit home. By the end of 1915 it became clear to the War Office that more recruitment was required. The solution was the Derby Scheme. Under this, men attested with a signed certificate, agreeing to enlist when called. Naturally, many thought that the war would be over before they were called, and they were wrong.

John Graham, the official historian of the NCF, put the situation strongly: 'The War Office had drained the country of all willing men who could be at all reasonably spared. But it was now represented to be a choice between defeat and a force so vastly increased that conscription was the only way to collect it.' Derby's attestation was in effect a compiled register. First, unmarried men between eighteen and forty-one were called; then later married men were included. As Graham put it, 'The nation had come to believe that every available man must be compelled to join up.'

A parliamentary furore was destined to happen when the first Military Service Act was introduced by Asquith of a coalition government, on 5 January 1916. The crucially important little word *deemed* was used. The aim was that all single men or widowers between the set ages were 'deemed' to have enlisted and should be conscripted into the Reserve. That meant that they would be recruited to a service battalion – one trained to be ready to replenish the numbers at the front after the usual heavy losses in battle. The result was that these men were actually defined as soldiers, without any process of proper induction. All that the Act stipulated concerning resisters was that they would not be given the death penalty (the usual punishment for disobeying orders in many circumstances) and that they would be placed before a civil court.

The debates that followed were mostly around the notion of exemption. The word was used a million times, and was to be used again and again across the land as tribunals were established. Clause 2 (3) explained the exemption appeal process:

> Any certificate of exemption may be absolute, conditional or temporary, as the authority by whom it was granted think best suited to the case. In cases of exemption on conscientious grounds the tribunal decision may take the form of an exemption from combatant service only, or may be conditional on the applicant being engaged on some work which in the opinion of the tribunal dealing with the case is of national importance.

This was the foundation of the thinking behind the bill. Then came the first reading, and this was opposed by Sir John Simon. He argued that the tribunals simply would not function as envisaged; he saw that the case of the average CO would be very unlikely to withstand examination based on existing prejudice. He was indeed prescient. Behind him was the Quaker line of thought, and for that, Arnold Rowntree spoke. He raised the topic of the ambulance unit, which he pointed out some Quaker friends had already discussed. Other speakers followed, raising various issues which they foresaw would make COs particularly vulnerable.

There was still concern about the death penalty. The King's Regulations at that time (and still) was a solid volume, thick with lists, exceptions, and most of all, with legal syntax and unwieldy clauses in lengthy sentences. The idea of punishment was everywhere, as of course an army has to operate by fear and respect, so that its essential hierarchy is maintained. Philip Snowden now enters the picture in this respect. He had studied the Army Act, Section XII (1) and saw that a CO would need protection from any strict application of that dreadful penalty.

Philip Snowden's political career spanned more than forty years, and in that time his fortunes and popularity swayed from hugely successful to almost rock bottom. At the centre of his beliefs, after he developed into a socialist from beginnings in the Liberal movement, was the concept of ethical socialism. This was a belief that, in order to change the lives of everyone in all echelons in society for the better, moral views and actions were needed, but they could only happen if the economic basis of industrial society changed. That angle on political matters was to lead him into being a pacifist when such opinions were discredited, and further a feminist, albeit one who upset some of the suffragette leaders.

The foundations of his politics were in the life he knew in Keighley and in his home village of Ickornshaw near Cowling. But a glance at the main events and influences in his life shows some admirable achievements for a boy born into a Wesleyan family in a northern weaving village. He was MP for Blackburn in 1906 and for Colne Valley in 1922; he was Chancellor of the Exchequer in

Ramsay MacDonald's 1923 government, the first Labour one, and was still Chancellor in the later national government of 1931.

We know a great deal about Snowden's early life and about his developing interest in the political ideologies which shaped his consciousness; we know these things from his own writing, as he published his autobiography in 1934. He was born on 18 July 1864 at Ickornshaw, and his family were Methodists with strong beliefs in education; Philip was at school in Cowling and also attended the Wesleyan Sunday School. He entered the world of work as a clerk in the insurance business. As a youth, he came to know the life and relationships around the world of work in a typical Yorkshire textiles community and he came to know nearby Keighley as well.

Many of his beliefs were grounded in a syncretic kind of morality which fused the Temperance Movement and the kind of radicalism he would have found in the Chartist movement. He actually met and listened to some of the famous Chartists and he wrote about some of them; closer to home his own father was involved in that movement. Snowden wrote, 'I have heard my father relate how a number of handloom weavers contributed a halfpenny a week to buy a copy of the weekly *Leeds Mercury*, which was then seven pence, and with these coppers he was sent to a village four miles away.'

But it was education in the age of self-help that made Snowden well equipped for politics and along with his development as a speaker, he was soon acquiring the kind of knowledge a man needed then to talk and to be heard and respected. He explains his education after the 1870 Education Act in complimentary terms: 'The walls were covered with maps and pictures. Our curriculum was extended to include grammar, geography, history, elementary mathematics and the simple sciences ... We were not troubled with the religious question.'

From 1895, Snowden became notably active in promulgating the new Labour gospel, going on a long and arduous lecture tour – even visiting Scotland and Wales. When he came to campaign to enter parliament, he did not look prepossessing but clearly had drive and energy. One account of him in 1907 describes him as 'small of stature and frail of frame, with a limp that compels him to lean heavily on a stick as he walks, he regards the world unblinkingly out of a pair of piercing eyes deep-sunken beneath an overhanging brow ...' But he was a very talented public speaker and was counted to be on a par with Keir Hardie in that respect. He had a religious aspect as well, with talks titled such as, 'The Christ that is to be', and he gave a dimension of religious revivalism to his extant socialism. In 1898 he was editor of the *Keighley Labour Journal*; the foundations of his life work were there in journalism and politics, the former providing a steady and respectable station, even if the politics failed.

After failures early in the new century, he finally won the seat of Blackburn in 1906; the people must have recalled him from his energetic first attempt to woo their votes in 1900. Blackburn was Tory at the time and, as David James has written, Snowden 'mesmerised the electors of Blackburn. In ten days he swept Socialism from obscurity into a position which made it a serious contender for power.' Even with over seven thousand votes, he lost in 1900. But in 1906 he was Labour MP for the town. By that time he was also writing books on his politics. Christian Socialism was the key concept, and in books such as *The Socialist Budget* (1907) and *Socialism and the Drink Question* (1908) he showed that he had a sense of the practical nous needed to link party doctrine to wider issues of how life was to be lived with an intrinsic moral worth.

Snowden was a marked pacifist, for which he lost much support and sympathy, of course. His personal life also played a part in his increasingly controversial position with regard to his political stance; his wife Ethel, whom he married in 1905, was an active campaigner for women's suffrage as well as for temperance reform. He began a worldwide lecture tour on the outbreak of war, and so avoided some of the worst repercussions of his outspoken pacifism and views on the war with Germany. When he was back in England, he did not hold back from expressing his opinions about militarism and warmongers. For him, the ILP was more important than the war machine; he made enemies of course but lost a certain degree of trust even within the Labour movement.

In this debate, Snowden reiterated that his fears regarding the death penalty were not an expression of any individual paranoid temperament, and when F. E. Smith pointed out that the War Office would never inflict such a penalty on men, Snowden was not reassured. He pointed out that the fear lay in the nature of the tribunals: if those panels found men to be insincere ('shirkers') then those people were open to all kinds of abuses – even to a death penalty being imposed. But there was a clause in the Act which, in the words of Harvey, who was the official historian of the NCF, 'excused the CO from the death penalty for refusing to obey the call to the colours' but, he added, 'It was, however, held afterwards that this excuse only covered the initial refusal and left the persistent objector liable to a death sentence after his forcible inclusion in the Army.'

At this juncture in the debate over the first reading, enter William Joynson-Hicks. At the time he was MP for Brentwood, and he was a formidable opponent, taking reactionary stances regarding any refusal to fight on the part of Englishmen. He was born William Hicks in 1865, and he became a solicitor. His attitude to the war was defined by the fact that he had established a Pals' battalion as part of the Middlesex Regiment – later to be called 'the footballers' battalion.

During the mid-months of 1916, Joynson-Hicks became a terrier for the cause of conscription, speaking in the House on several occasions with regard to potential sources of manpower. He sniffed out available men in all kinds of places, including, in June of that year, eligible men in government departments. The *Hansard* report reads:

Mr Johnson-Hicks asked the Prime Minister whether he will consent to the appointment of a small committee of this House to enquire into the necessity for further combing out of men of military age in Government Departments?

The Prime Minister: No, Sir, I do not think it would be desirable to adopt this proposal, and I would refer the Hon. Member to the speech of my Right Hon. Friend the Financial Secretary to the Treasury on the Motion ...

Mr Joynson-Hicks: Will the Right Hon. Gentleman see that the House has an opportunity of considering and debating the very important return which has been issued showing the number of men still in Government employ?

The Prime Minister: I think there will be many opportunities for doing that.

Joynson-Hicks had already asked for an estimate of the numbers of officers across the land who were engaged in recruiting offices;

he wanted them to be taken into combat zones as well. There was no surprise, then, when he proposed that the exemptions should be given only to Quakers or members of other religious bodies which include an objection to all war among their fundamental tenets. Harvey summarised Joynson-Hicks' attitude: 'He called the clause the Slackers' Charter, was satirical at great length about these shirkers, would have liked to have had no exemption clause' but was willing to accept 'clearly definable bodies of a religious character.'

All this discussion was largely based on a common opinion that large numbers of young men had suddenly and rather conveniently acquired pacifist religious principles at the outbreak of war. With this in mind, Joynson-Hicks suggested that immunity to conscription should apply only to people who were members of the Society of Friends as at 5 August 1914.

Johnson-Hicks' suggested amendments were refused. It was then that T. Edmund Harvey, a pacifist, made a speech of great rhetorical and moral persuasion. The heart of his argument ventured into philosophy, placed well away from any immediate reference to the war: 'We profoundly believe that the soldier and the military system belong to a stage of society in which war will be a thing of the past.' But when the debate was opened up again, the familiar lines of thought from the belligerent majority reasserted themselves, perhaps being most crudely expressed by Mr Chaplin: 'Every man who prefers to love his enemies at this time is unworthy of the name of Englishman.'

There was then an apparent turn, urged by the Home Secretary, Herbert Samuel. The NCF supporters thought that this was an optimistic element in the political to and fro of the debate, particularly when he said, 'We want to give the widest possible latitude ... But the honourable member says the effect of the government's proposal is that his friend would have forced upon him, by the requirements of the Tribunal, some particular kind of work. Surely that is what he himself proposes.' This was reassuring because the average CO wanted to be given some alternative work, something that did not directly support the military actions.

An amendment was then suggested which would have had a statement on oath by a CO made before two justices of the peace, but this was summarily rejected. But at least, before the vote, it was pointed out that there were ten thousand members of the NCF and that there would inevitably be a great deal of unfairness in the behaviour of the tribunals.

The vote was highly in favour of the bill, and it was soon before the House of Lords. No amendments were allowed, and it was then a case of working out practicalities. These included actions related to drafting objectors into munitions work; medical rejects were to be enrolled at labour exchanges, and an improvised and alternative route of industrial conscription was evolved. But the old duress was still there, as with one member who told the House of a Dundee employer who, confronted with striking workers, promptly reported them to the Army to have them dragged into regular conscription.

John Graham, who had recounted all these political events, offered his own assessment of the coming tribunals, and gave a survey of the problems he foresaw:

One often wondered, when moving among the machinery of compulsion, noting the piles of printed forms, and the armies of clerks attached to the tribunals, the laborious court martials, the increase in the population of the gaols and detention in barracks and their costs, the illness and enfeeblement of the victims, the great waste of all kinds of skill among the young men, besides the ruin of businesses ... whether on the whole, conscription had been worthwhile, on a purely military valuation.

The Act was passed by a large majority, but it is significant that the TUC voted on the bill, and the result was 541,000 for and 2,121,000 against; the Miners' Federation's vote was 38,000 for the bill and 653,190 against. There were also resolutions made against conscription by the War Emergency Workers' National Committee, by the Scottish Labour Party, the Welsh miners and the National Executive of Locomotive Engineers and Firemen.

However, the lists of parliamentarians who were for peace has some interesting inclusions: among the most famous were Ramsay McDonald, Viscount Simon, Philip Snowden and Viscount Morley; these were joined by the 2nd Earl Russell (Bertrand Russell's grandfather) and even Lord Courtney of Penwith. Altogether, there were fifty-two men sympathetic to the CO cause.

There was a meeting at the Fabian Rooms in Tothill Square in which the NCF, the Society of Friends and the Fellowship of Reconciliation met. They decided on a deputation to the House of Commons, and they took as their collective name the National Council Against Conscription. Among them was Sylvia Pankhurst, who wrote one of the most comprehensive accounts of the home front during the war, and she was indeed a worthy addition to that deputation. She and other women joined the group, with her recalling, 'We passed, a little irregular stream of us, along the pavement to the House; mainly bourgeois, middle-aged and elderly, black lace mantles and black silk skirts trailing and rustling.' She concluded that they pleaded but to no avail. However, at least the crisis brought forward a number of talented men and women who were to play significant roles in the agitation against conscription. There may not have been any immediately positive or encouraging responses to the pleas made, but at least the Council Against Conscription had been formed, led by Robert Smillie, F. W. Pethick Lawrence and Langdon Davies. Smillie was president; he was born in Belfast in 1878, the son of a crofter, before he was orphaned, then being brought up by his grandmother. As a child, his first work was in a spinning mill, and he became what so many socialist and radical leaders were at that time – an autodidact, reading widely, and learning piecemeal, but doggedly and successfully. In his early teens he went to Scotland and worked in the Larkhall mines, still furthering his education as and when he could. In 1885 he became secretary of the Larkhall Miners' Association, and then progressed to be a founding member of the Scottish Labour Party in 1888, and then similarly again of the ILP in 1893. In the early phase of the war, he campaigned to keep the miners out of the purview of the Munitions Act, and concomitant to that effort was his energy devoted to opposing conscription in general.

Sylvia continued her account of the meetings with Smillie and others: 'We met in a bare little office in Bride Lane ... Our Federation members were there each day pleading with the Labour men to stand by their pledges.' With the passing of the Act imminent, the NCF issued a statement:

Freedom of conscience must not be sacrificed to military necessity ... Men's deepest religious and moral convictions must not be swept aside. We believe in human brotherhood. We will not kill. We will accept no military duties. While the soul of Britain lives, our witness cannot be in vain.

The one apparently positive element in the passage of the bill was Asquith's promise that the widows' only sons would not be conscripted. He said, 'When there is a single unmarried son left behind it would of course be a monstrous thing if the State were to call for military service from a man in that position.' He did what many statesmen through the ages have done to back up the promise – he quoted Shakespeare, speaking these lines from *Henry V*:

> Go 'cruit me Cheshire and Lancashire
> And Derby hills that are so free.
> No married man or widow's son,
> No widow's curse shall go with me.

But the Military Service Act was created, and what followed was the establishment of the tribunals. The members of these courts (which, in effect, are what they were) were chosen from lists sent from political groups. The people sitting were a mix of elderly magistrates, with an Army representative, and some legal professionals. Tribunals had previously been brought into use and convened, working to deal with the attested men under the Derby Scheme, but now many more were called. A government circular was distributed, written by John Long, and the crucially important statement therein was something that every CO would have wanted to see written down. It was, however, to be ignored: 'Whatever may be the views of members of the tribunal, they must interpret the Act in an impartial and tolerant spirit. Difference of convictions must not bias judgment.'

C. H. Norman, a member of the NCF, wrote a critique of these tribunals which is borne out by the records and testimonies associated with their practice, as we shall see later in this chapter. Norman wrote:

Members of the Local and Appeal Tribunals possessed no special qualification for their duties, beyond being men of some position in local politics. The Act was administered with much favouritism and much harshness, especially in the case of applicants on domestic, business and health grounds. The man who carried on his little business was swept into the Army ... The man who was the sole support of his aged mother or father was taken away ... The man who was ailing received little consideration from the Tribunals ... until the scandals of the Army medical boards so aroused public indignation that such men had their medical history examined into somewhat carefully at the Tribunals, before being remitted to the Army medical boards.

The outcome was that all the important decisions were left to the tribunals. Many were smarting from the defeat of the opposition, but some odd consequences occurred, such as the Labour Party's refusal, stated at their conference, to agitate for the repeal of the Act. As to the pledge not to immediately enlist married men, that was forgotten within days of the legislation being passed. Sylvia Pankhurst noted, '"Married shirkers next!" shrieked The Regiment, a bellicose little paper which presumed to express the Army point of view.' One journalist summed up the awful result of the Act, 'By means of grading and putting into categories, the men have been tricked and cajoled to get into the Army.'

Soon after the Act was passed, it has to be noted that the press gave more than the usual column space to pacifist events. In January, what stood out was the violent row at Devonshire House in Bishopsgate, when Charles Buxton tried to give a lunchtime talk on 'The War – Problems of Settlement'. As he rose to speak, a man called Richard Glover, of the Anti-German Union, shouted out, 'You're trying to teach pro-Germanism under the cloak of religion!' The main accusation was that the speaker belonged to the Union of Democratic Control, which was generally a middle-of-the-road pacifist group. When Buxton admitted that he was, Glover called out, 'Then you are a dirty traitor!' Buxton said outright that it was time for concessions to be made to the Germans, and then they in turn would make concessions. His continued attempts to insist that Germany could be trusted to cooperate in peace talks only served to raise the ire against him. Someone spoke from among the crowd, 'What do you care about the Empire? I would not insult the country by calling you an Englishman. The man who won't fight for his country ought to be hanged, and that is what you will come to.' When Buxton thanked him, the man in the crowd replied 'He seems very pleased' and there was general laughter.

That kind of publicity for the pacifist cause in general served a dual purpose. First, it kept the CO debate going in the face of conscription, and second, it reminded the general reader that there was a wide spectrum of debate and a range of organisations involved in non-combatant activity.

*

The tribunals were soon running efficiently, and the call went out to unmarried men at first, telling them to present themselves ready for becoming fighting men. A few writers did at least point out at this juncture that men who had been passed as medically unfit were still receiving these orders. The stage was set for a long and bitter series of tribunal confrontations, at which the categories were to be sorted out – decisions that created rulings for complete exemption, non-combatant service, temporary exemption, or drafting into the Army to be immediately put into action. But the underlying legal system also included the possibility of a transfer to an appeal tribunal from the local one.

There is no shortage of information about the tribunals, despite the fact that tribunal records were ordered to be destroyed in the 1920s. The public could attend the local ones, and Sylvia Pankhurst reported on such an occasion, at Bethnal Green, writing that the appeals of four COs were heard and rejected. She summed up the other applicants and their destinies before the panel:

> Amongst other applicants was a small greengrocer and furniture remover, who pleaded for total exemption to carry on his business, as the sole support of an aged father, two widowed sisters and their children. He was brusquely allowed a month's exemption to wind up his affairs before joining the regiment. Jews were treated even more relentlessly than other applicants; the destruction of their small businesses seemed to give a real satisfaction to the tribunal.

This is an interesting aspect of the tribunal business. Pankhurst's isolating of the anti-Jewish feeling among the members of the supposed impartial tribunal panel hints at the nature of the power given to these members, whose actions often assert the truth of Shakespeare's lines in *Measure for Measure*: 'Man, proud man, dressed in a little brief authority ... plays such fantastic tricks before high heaven/ as make the angels weep.' Her point is borne out in the case of Leeds, a city with a large Jewish population. The local newspapers reported regularly throughout the end of 1915 and the first months of 1916, on whether or not the Jewish citizens were 'doing their bit' and enlisting. The persistent and recurrent problem of Jewish immigrants across the world was in focus; namely posing the issue with renewed interest as to their possibly being fully integrated to an extent that they think, feel and act like a man whose expressions of patriotism and national allegiance are compatible with an uprooted ethnicity. Through our modern eyes, the reporting on the matter was disgusting – a type of victimisation. But the anti-Semitism was apparent in 1915–16, and it became pointed when Leeds people wanted the reassurance that the Jewish citizens were doing what everyone else was doing – joining up.

The Yorkshire Post ran a feature headed, 'An Able Defence of the Jews: Has he done his bit? – one reason why anti-Semitic feeling is running high.' The paper expressed a spirited response to the critics of the Jewish population:

> In Leeds there is a Jew-baiting coterie such as exists nowhere else in this country. It consists chiefly of property owners and some of their tenants, who boycott the Jew simply because he is a Jew. The English-born Jew, the Jew who is eligible for the Army, resents and cannot understand these petty discriminations. There is another aspect of this subject which is frequently overlooked by those who embark upon anti-Jewish propaganda. There are many Jewish homes in Leeds today where Armageddon has exacted heavy toll, and where Jewish women are trying to console themselves that their men folk went under in defence of Britain's honour.

In spite of the destruction of tribunal records, we have a remarkably intact knowledge of their function from memoirs and anecdotes. There are very few accounts in fiction, but there is one notable exception – a novel called *The Bustling Hours* by W. Pett Ridge, published in 1919. He has this description of the setting for a tribunal hearing:

> The dozen men, in a semi-circle at one end of a large room, sat back and gazed at the ceiling or allowed their eyes to glance at portraits on the wall. One or two sipped a very early cup of tea and munched toast. The clerk, rising, said the next was Charles Pritchard, classed as B2, one-man business, bookseller and newsagent of 79, High Street, St. John's Wood, aged 32, married; one child. The military representative said that B2 men were urgently wanted.

The novel has, as part of the storyline, the plot that the applicant's mother knows a lawyer who is on the panel, and she arranges for a solution to the problem.

The lack of official records has been replaced in part by a plethora of newspaper reports across the shires, and by memoirs. In these we find sidelights, and of course, rare insights. For instance, in a self-published memoir written by J. Barlow Brooks, a Methodist minister working on Connor's Quay at the outbreak of war, we have an account of the kind of bullying and prejudice that filtered through the system. Brooks was a pacifist, and expressed his opinions strongly:

> Many Christian leaders and members of our churches acquiesce in war, and many openly advocate it when war breaks out as unavoidable. Though obviously Christ taught the opposite, they try to argue that he favoured it by quoting that he scourged the money-lenders out of the Temple ... as if that single incident compared with the wholesale massacre of men, women and children. So millions die to maintain the sway of plutocrats over the dispossessed.

All the more surprising, then, that Brooks was asked to be a member of the Connor's Quay tribunal. He notes that the panel was composed of a churchman, a Labour representative, Captain Hughes (a retired soldier), Brooks himself and the military man, Captain Marriott. He remarked that the Labour man wanted to 'send all unmarried men to the front ... He was unmarried'. Brooks points out that he read all the latest directives and regulations sent from London to the tribunals, and so he had a sound knowledge of procedure. But something happened which was happening everywhere: a government man from elsewhere arrived – in this case from Chester – to veto decisions made. Brooks wrote: 'Things went fairly smoothly until the country got the wind up and men began to be taken regardless of their physical condition.'

The man from Chester (Captain S.) tried to bully the panel into the 'right' decisions, such as in the cases where there had been previous decisions to refuse exemption. Brooks isolates one typical case and recounts how the tribunal found a way to subvert the interloper's hectoring intrusion:

There were several straightforward cases and then Captain S. intervened.

'... This man's in the Army. You can't deal with him. Here's the decision. He was refused exemption at Rhyl. You must dismiss the case. We will look after him.'

' ... Perhaps you will read particulars of the Rhyl application,' said the chairman.

' ... You're wasting my valuable time. I have to go by the 4.30 train,' said the official irritably.

Then Captain Hughes, who had been growing restive, spoke. 'The Captain is at liberty to go whenever he likes. We have no train to catch and we shall be able to transact the business of the tribunal without his assistance.'

The applicant finally won his appeal, largely because the panel wasted time, so that the visitor had to catch his train.

Another insight into the tribunals comes from Barlow Brooks: his tribunal went on strike. The reason for this was that their decisions had been overturned by a tribunal at Mold. The head official for North Wales eventually came to meet them and the cases in question were looked at. Typical was the case of a young man who had had several operations on one eye and was in danger of losing his sight. Men like that, clearly unfit for military service, were being bullied into recruitment. The strikers won the day. Brooks adds, with a dash of humour, that the administrator told them to write to the War Office, and the comment is, 'We laughed at this advice ... and said that the war would be over before we got a reply from the circumlocution office in London.'

*

Something far more serious was happening as these tribunals carried on. In May of that year, a group of COs who had been refused exemption were, in consequence, deemed to be in the Army, and so were taken over to France. This was a nasty warning of what might happen, as they were technically serving soldiers and so now subject to the discipline of the King's Regulations. The discussion in the House when the Military Service Act was being processed, as we have seen, touched on the death penalty for disobedience. Despite assurances to the contrary, the possibility of that punishment still loomed. There were also lesser punishments, but these also were horrendous. They were known as field punishments 1 and 2. There

had long been brutal physical punishment applied in the Army –
flogging had been allowed until as recently as 1881. But the field
punishments were to remain in force until 1923. The first entailed the
prisoner being tied up in pain for a long period, as one CO recalled:

> The Quartermaster Sergeant had us each handcuffed to a tent with
> our hands round the pole behind us, which made the shoulders ache
> to a quite excruciating degree. The young Canadian, who had been
> so hostile the previous evening, came up. He broke into a torrent
> of curses at the authorities who imposed such penalties. After three
> hours, one of the handcuffs was unlocked to enable me to feed
> myself, after which the punishment was again inflicted.

Field punishment number 2 involved the man being shackled,
but not to any fixed object. This act of tying and fixing a man to
something was rather ironically nicknamed a 'crucifixion':

> We were placed with our faces to the barbed wire of the inner fence.
> As the ropes with which we were tied fastened round the barbed
> wire instead of the usual thick wooden post it was possible to tie
> them much more tightly, and I found myself drawn so closely to
> the fence that when I wished to turn my head I had to do so very
> cautiously to avoid my face being torn by the barbs.

With this kind of regime in mind, we find that the men sent across
the Channel in May were extremely vulnerable. Nowhere was
any decree in force on paper, that the death penalty would not be
imposed. Thirty-seven men were taken, shipped from camps at
Harwich and Richmond, and thirty of these men received the death
sentence. The NCF only found out this fact when the prisoners

were already in transit. They were bound for Southampton, and the NCF tried to contact them. A group of seventeen COs, from the Harwich group, began to refuse orders. The field punishments followed, and finally the men were all moved abroad and then stationed at Boulogne. A campaign accelerated from home, and missives were sent to MPs and others. The Joint Advisory Council of the NCF saw that it was imperative that a representative be sent to Boulogne. The man chosen was Dr F. B. Meyer.

At this point, it seems clear that Meyer was shown by the officers in charge only what they wanted him to see. Meyer spoke briefly to a few COs, but was always accompanied by senior staff. The crucially important time had come. Here there were these men, who had technically mutinied in the eyes of martial law. It was a serious breach of morale and regulations. The thirty men in question had been court-martialled and their fate hung in the balance. They had not been 'read out' – meaning that their death sentence had not yet been declared openly. Then matters advanced decisively, as the diary of one of the COs recounts:

On Monday, the 9 June, we were informed we were to be read out. We found an escort awaiting us in the courtyard below ... We turned towards the outskirts of the town and climbed one of the hills overlooking it, which afforded a wide view of the Channel. I cast many a glance in the direction of the white cliffs of Dover, for this might be our last opportunity. We turned into the midst of a huge military camp and many curious eyes, evidently puzzled by our cheerful demeanour ... After a wait of perhaps three quarters of an hour ... an appropriate hush had been arranged, and the adjutant who was to read out the sentence took charge. 'Private —— No —— of the 2nd Eastern Company Non-Combatant Corps ... for

disobedience while undergoing field punishment ... sentenced to
death by being shot.' Here a pause ... 'Confirmed by General Sir
Douglas Haig ... and commuted to ten years penal servitude.'

One soldier recalled later, 'These men aren't normal. Look at the
shape of their heads! Colonel Wilberforce has said to me in a
friendly discussion before we left Boulogne.'

*

There were thirty men on the death list. The historian of the NCF
wrote later, 'With the men condemned to death rests the honour
and glory of standing steadfast and unflinching in the very front of
the struggle for a new normality and a higher convention.'

Questions were asked in the House. There was a heated debate
on 26 June, in which once again Philip Snowden took part. Mr
Wing started the discussion with a request that a different method
be found of dealing with COs, and the prime minister promised a
speech on that the following day. But there followed expressions
of outrage at such an un-English matter as a death sentence in
those circumstances. Mr Edmund Harvey spoke directly; with no
embellishment; he asked the Prime Minister, 'Whether his attention
has been called to the court-martial held at Boulogne upon
Howard Marten, a member of the Society of Friends, and three
other conscientious objectors to military service, at which the court
sentenced these men to death by shooting: whether this sentence
was subsequently commuted to ten years penal servitude ... and
whether any steps are to be taken to prevent any similar action
by courts-martial in future?' Asquith struggled to say anything
of any substance. He met angry questions and utter outrage, as
several MPs took the opportunity to describe horrendous instances

of cruelty, such as Mr Whitehouse's question regarding C. H. Norman, who was confined in Wandsworth Detention Barracks. He asked, 'Whether, on 23 May, he was confined in a straightjacket, which was too small and caused him great agony; whether the then commandant, who has since been removed, mocked at him; whether Mr Norman fainted and was left unconscious on the floor for an hour; whether he was afterwards taken to hospital; and whether he returned to the barracks on 31 May and was again subjected to brutality by the then commandant?'

The events in Boulogne highlighted for all the horrendous cruelty imposed on the men who would not fight. It was noticed that Meyer's presence at Boulogne had been left out of any reference, and Mr King asked if Meyer's report had been seen by those in power. He noted that Meyer had spoken to fourteen of the prisoners and had commented that they had been on a bread and water diet for some time. Meyer, a Baptist preacher, born in 1847, was highly respected; he preached at Christ Church, London, and one man who knew him said that 'Meyer preaches as a man who has seen God face to face'. His report would have been thorough and honest. But the response from Harold Tennant, Financial Secretary to the War Office, was, 'No Sir. No report by the Revd F. B. Meyer has been submitted to the War Office and I was unaware that he had prepared any report.'

One batch of men sent to France then was the resisters who had been placed in Richmond Castle. On the wall of a cell there are written these words: '"I" Percy F. Goldsbrough of Mirfield was brought up from Pontefract on Friday, 11 August 1916 and put into this cell for refusing to be made into a soldier.' The group there became known as the 'Richmond Sixteen' and they were a mixed collection of faiths, including Quakers, Methodists and members of the Church of Christ. The men there were absolutists, and among them were a professional footballer, Norman Gaudie, who played for Sunderland, and Bert Brocklesby, a Quaker who memorably wrote, as war broke out, 'However many might volunteer yet I would not ... God has not put me on earth to go destroying his own children.'

Brocklesby was a particularly interesting speaker and writer. He was born in Conisborough near Doncaster in 1889, and although he began as a Methodist, he became a Quaker and was based at the Scunthorpe Meeting. He was twenty-seven in 1914 and did not keep his conscience to himself, as he preached against war and refused to be conscripted. Hence his destination was prison, and he was incarcerated with the Richmond group at Boulogne. He was later sent to Dyce Camp (which will figure in the next chapter) and, after release in 1919, he became a teacher, in which role he worked first in Africa and then at home in Scunthorpe.

The Richmond Sixteen were classified as non-combatants and were put with the 2nd Northern Company of Non-Combatants, at Richmond Castle. They refused to wear any uniforms and so were placed in solitary confinement in small cells.

In the chronicle of the Boulogne 'reading out' incident the Richmond group will always figure prominently, because one of the group wrote a letter to Arnold Rowntree, MP for York; and although the author threw the letter out of the train as the group were taken south, it did actually reach Rowntree, who then spoke to the prime minister, Asquith, about the matter.

The details of the destinations of the Richmond Sixteen do not make happy reading: in July 1917, Alfred Martlew was found drowned in the River Ouse, and although the others were freed in 1919, they always had to live with the stigma of being thought of as cowards, and they were further disenfranchised for five years. Their time in Richmond is now marked by a spot called the Cockpit Garden, a memorial to them.

*

The tribunals went on. Repeatedly, the same issues were seen across every judgment made in Britain: the overbearing influence of the military presence, the susceptibility of the panels to local bias and influence, and above all, the lack of any genuine effort to understand the arguments given to them by a whole range of applicants. The latter fell roughly into three categories: the COs, the people in business and the medical or humanitarian cases. The last category called for human understanding and a degree of empathy, and in most of the extensive chronicles of tribunal reportage this quality was notably missing. Too often the strongest, most forceful individual (usually the Army man) won the day and the most subtle and most nuanced of arguments were dismissed without proper consideration. There were exceptions of course, but when gathering together the witness statements and reports, there is no doubt that prejudice and intolerance were systemic.

This may be seen in a cogently argued article written by Eva Gore-Booth after seeing a tribunal in progress. At this time she was forty-six and known as a poet and writer; she had also created the Sligo branch of the Irish Women's Suffrage Association. She wrote her analysis just after the Easter Rising in Ireland, in which her sister had received a sentence of death, though it was later commuted. A strong influence on her was the sinking of the *Lusitania* in 1915, and she gave a lecture at a conference on the Pacifist Philosophy of Life. This was headed 'Religious Aspects of Non-Resistance'. She met and impressed both Brockway and

Bertrand Russell, and her views on the Military Service Act were expressed in a letter to the Manchester Guardian in which she wrote, 'May I point out that, as the bill now stands, if a man fails to convince a committee nominated by the local authority not only that he is a bona fide conscientious objector, but also that a conscientious objector should be exempted, he may pay with his life for the private militarist views of members of his district council.'

The strength of her feeling in this matter runs through her report on the tribunal. She began by summarising a pathetic case of an old and infirm man who had a small tailoring business, and one son had already gone to war; the remaining son was needed for the business, and of course, to care for his father. Eva Gore-Booth saw that he was obviously 'frail and broken', and she adds, 'For a moment one felt sure that even these men, with their merciless mania for destruction, must feel a touch of human sympathy and understanding.' But no, the reply the old man had received from the Army representative was 'We want that man', and his son was doomed to be a soldier.

Eva Gore-Booth described three types of CO. These were the nervous type, the quiet and determined sort and finally the one capable of putting forth a philosophical argument. They all, as she watched the proceedings, failed to attain the status of exemption. Her report assigns plenty of blame for narrow-mindedness and prejudice on the churchmen present. In the case of a man asked by the churchman the commonest question given to a CO – 'If your mother was attacked by a German with a bayonet, would you not kill him to save your mother's life?' – the man's response was clever, well versed in Christian thinking, and therefore seen as obstinate and annoying by the panel. The applicant said, after asking if the churchman believed in God, 'Well, if that is so, do you not think my mother's life would be safer in His hands than in mine, stained with my brother's blood?'

There was no real answer. Eva Gore-Booth captured in this piece arguably the most solidly argued and most vivid account of the intractable difficulties faced by COs in the dock.

The situation with the tribunals and the determined effort to enforce conscription whenever possible was further stirred and fomented by the national and regional press. The *Yorkshire Post*, for instance, in December 1915, when the topic of attestation and the 'Derby Men' was hot news, made no mistake that it saw a certain group in the Leeds community who were not pulling their weight:

> It is no use blinking the fact that the bachelors of Roundhay, Chapeltown and Headingley, particularly those between 20 and 30 years of age, stand exposed as a race apart from the patriotic Englishman. The rich and the poor have proved their mettle, but I regret to say that the single men in a great number of middle-class families have shown themselves to be shirkers. It is the middle-classes who have brought the country to the need for compulsion.

One of the most heart-breaking stories of the tribunals relates to George Lansbury and his efforts on behalf of a London boy of eighteen whose mother, in the words of Sylvia Pankhurst, had experienced extreme hardship, 'Her struggle to rear her children, and especially this youngest, her only boy, had been tremendous. She had given her life for them, throb by throb; she was drained and spent.' George Lansbury was appealed to, and he applied himself to the case on behalf of the dispossessed defendant.

Lansbury was at the time the editor of the *Daily Herald*, and his paper had campaigned against the war from the outset. He was born in Suffolk in 1859, and even when very young he had realised the evil and waste of war. As a young boy he had argued on the futility of the Franco-Prussian War back in 1870; then in the atmosphere of jingoism for the Boer War in 1900 he stood as a socialist in the 'Khaki election'. He was also a supporter of women's suffrage and even stood for parliament as a 'Votes for Women' candidate. He had strong links to Bow, and was later to campaign for the issue of levying rates there.

In 1916, after being contacted by Sylvia, he met the boy's mother. Sylvia wrote that the mother was 'white and tragic, well-nigh speechless in her agony, ill and shivering in a bleak wind'. She was from Bow, and so Lansbury had a special interest. The plan was to have him employed in Bow as a labourer in a yard, and to plead that his work was 'essential', and so he would be a reserved man.

It was all to no avail. When the inevitable moment came when he would have to enlist, the worst thing happened. He left with the intention of joining a mechanics' corps, with the intention of at least avoiding the front line's action, but he returned home having been enlisted as an infantryman. Sylvia recounts an event shortly after that:

He was swiftly trained, swiftly indeed … The last time he was home on leave before going to France there was an air raid. He went out into the road. His mother cried to him, 'Come in! You will be killed.'

'I would rather be killed here, mother, than out there!' he answered her sadly.

The tragic but by no means exceptional end of the story is that he was reported missing, later officially 'presumed dead'. Lansbury carried on the fight to try to help those who were vulnerable to the thoughtless, inhumane actions of the tribunals. Though he suffered many setbacks, he fought and made his presence felt whenever he could. When a scheme to save a man called Whitelock, again in Bow, failed, a Major Rothschild sat at the Guildhall tribunal that refused the man exemption. Lansbury stood, and he roared, 'Shame on you Rothschild! Herbert Samuel has said that a moral objection is as good as a religious objection! You ought to be ashamed of yourself!'

Sometimes the tribunals were the scenes of extreme uproar and disorder, as was the case at Huddersfield on 25 March 1916. *The Worker* reporter set the scene: 'An air of excitement was noticeable from the outset' and 'so large was the attendance that scores had to stand through the afternoon, and the crowd extended into the corridors.' The interest lay in the person of Arthur Gardiner, a 'popular socialist protagonist'.

The large crowd made a noise all the way through an attempt by the Mayor, on the bench, to have the hearing done in private. Even worse, there were suggestions voiced that the panel had made a pre-arrangement as to what their decision would be regarding Gardiner's appeal. Then followed this interchange:

Mayor: I will not have any further discussion.
A Voice: We will be here all night then.
Another Voice: It is not a fair trial if it is in private.
A Voice: Can you throw us out without any help?

A woman questioned the right of the tribunal to turn out the public against the applicant's wishes.

A Voice: It is against the law.

Eventually the police arrived, but only after Gardiner had made a bargain that he would stay and the public would behave properly, as he had some influence with them. It was the Mayor's response that created further trouble:

Mayor: I have made my appeal for these people to retire. Now you shall make yours. On the first interruption I shall refuse to go on with the case, and you agree to go into another room to hear the case.

Gardiner then, at last, had leave to state his case, and he made a very impressive job of it, and *The Worker* reported it:

In his application, Gardiner said he was twenty-six years of age and was employed as a wool and cotton dyer. He could not conscientiously undertake combatant or non-combatant military service. For a number of years he had devoted his time and energy, both publicly and privately, to the economic and moral upliftment of humanity. He was opposed to all forms of militarism, believing it to be detrimental to the welfare of all nations.

The panel's response was summed up by the military member, Crosland: 'He has such curious ideas – they can't be worked out.' Then something fairly rare happened; the Mayor and Crosland fell out:

The Mayor: Oh yes, I am a member of the British Socialist Party and a member of the Socialist Sunday School.

Mr Crosland: I should refuse it. Whatever you do I shall oppose your decision.

The Mayor: That won't make the slightest difference.

Mr Crosland: It seems so foreign to have a man talk like he does.

The Mayor: I think I should like to retire.

They retired, and when they returned, the verdict was that the applicant was given two months' temporary exemption. Gardiner replied with, 'I shall have the right of appeal.'

*

What about the actual experience of being forced to become a soldier? What was it like to suddenly find that, regardless of your social standing and gentlemanly bearing, you were standing before a tribunal hell-bent on classifying you as a soldier, in spite of your insistence that you had a case for exemption based on conscience? Fortunately we have accounts written by excellent writers, professional men from a variety of spheres in society; a look at one as a case study will enlighten the subject. This is the case of Scott Duckers, a London lawyer, who found himself in the dock on several occasions, and then in military detention, still insisting that he was not in the Army and was not subject to a court martial. This was the situation of many such individuals, as their lives were transmuted from respectable members of respectable professions to the status of 'shirkers' in a strange kind of limbo, a purgatory outside of civil society.

Duckers' story exemplifies the limbo in which COs were placed when caught in the double bind of being assumed to be enlisted when, in fact and with evidence, they were still civilians, only then to be placed in a position of defence, relying on an alien system of military courts to hear their case fairly. In these circumstances, the possibility of such a fair hearing was mere fantasy, as Duckers' case proves.

He was arrested after his tribunal and from that point, after he had refused to take any part in the war, he was assumed to be a soldier and so under Army regulations. That meant, of course, that every time he disobeyed an order he had committed an offence and was once again in custody. As T. Edmund Harvey wrote in the preface to Duckers' memoir, printed in 1917, 'He is now in a civil prison. Yet he is still accounted in the eyes of the law a soldier.'

On 20 April 1916, Duckers stood before a court martial at Winchester. He was charged with refusing to follow a command. Duckers was defended by Horace Fenton, and Fenton found himself quibbling about terminology, in order that the charge could be placed in its rightful category of absurd. Duckers, when asked how he would plead, began by stating that he was not under military law. He had not actually said the words 'not guilty' as his plea, because he was not, in his view, a soldier. The result of this was that the officer in charge, Captain Judge, said that the issue was a plea about jurisdiction. That is, whether or not that court was allowed to apply process at all – given that the man in the dock was arguably not a soldier. The report in the local paper went on to detail, 'After further discussion the court was closed, and subsequently the President announced that they had come to the conclusion that the words which the accused had used, "I do not admit that I am under military law" was a direct challenge to the jurisdiction of the court ...' They asked him to plead yet again. What followed was certain to lead to his being returned to custody:

Mr Fenton: He is not bound to plead.

President: Then the court uses its powers and enters a plea of not guilty. I put the question again: was accused guilty or not guilty?

Accused: I have already pleaded, sir; I will not plead again.

President: Not guilty.

The talk went on, running through the supposed offence of not putting on military clothing. The argument went around and around, with nothing being achieved, and the result was an offer to attend a Central Tribunal. Doing that would have assumed that he was under military orders. The consequences of not attending were, in the words of the Central Tribunal of Westminster: 'If ... the tribunal are not satisfied that you have a conscientious objection to military service based on religious or moral grounds, you will be transferred to section W of the Army Reserve.'

*

All this persecution, with the requests for exemption's foregone conclusion of rejection, further led to men going absent – heading instead for some life of obscurity, anonymous and unknown. Sylvia Pankhurst looked at some of these cases and summed up the situation with the old crime-story phrase of *on the run*. The main gambit open to the fugitives was to hide in a sympathetic home. Sylvia Pankhurst wrote, for instance, 'Mrs —, one of our Bow members who had been in prison as a Suffragette, with the help of another member, a dressmaker living alone, succeeded in hiding her husband and brother-in-law until the war was over.'

This created a tense situation in which, at any place and at any time, a crowd could be subject to a random entrapment and search by soldiers or police, in order that COs on the run could be apprehended.

The search would sift evidence of identity, attestation forms, any evidence of exemption, and of course, for soldiers on leave. Such an event happened on 16 November at Holborn Hall, when there was an annual reunion held by the *Daily Herald*, with Lansbury speaking to the crowd. Two military officers arrived with a troop of soldiers and they rounded up for inspection anyone who was in their way. As they then guarded the doors, a large contingent of police officers came and papers were inspected. There were four young men present who knew that there was no escape. They were taken in, and it was recorded by one witness that 'A youth who was found to possess exemption papers was flung headforemost down the steps.'

When those who had kept themselves at home until the call-up came were finally called, their wish to avoid killing and being killed provided raw and heart-rending tales, as was the case with Fred Payne, who was recruited, then trained at camp. He ran off after bayonet training, horrified by the thought of administering such a brutal death to another human being. Sylvia Pankhurst describes what happened next:

> Half crazed with fear and horror, he broke away and sped back to his house. He slunk in like a thief ... quaking with fear at the sound of every footstep ... the old father in terror, bade him go back to camp ... Many a mile they led him, shuffling their old weary feet. His strength, sapped by cold fear, was less than theirs. They took his arms and dragged him on between them ... So on the threshold of the camp they left him-seeing him enter with his manhood crushed.

The root of their fear – the force that drove the parents to do this – was the thought that the father would be dragged off to prison if he harboured his fugitive son.

As must be expected, the press in almost all cases was merciless in its commentary on the activities of the COs, and the media generally took great pleasure in posting satirical representations of those who would not fight – especially the absolutists. One postcard depicted two COs with brushes and dustpans, being ridiculed by a line of Tommies in a trench with their guns firing. The caption read, 'While the shot and shell are flying and the mighty cannons boom, he is tidying up the trenches with a dust-pan and a broom.' Another card shows a line of German soldiers advancing towards three COs who have sheet music in their hands, and one sheet with the song title, *You Made Me Love You*. The caption reads, 'The gentlemen with consciences require no swords or guns – they're going to win the war by singing love songs to the Huns.' When it came to the concerns relating to the tribunals, the artists had an equally good time with this, too. One card, by the famous Donald McGill, shows a CO standing in front of a panel of four officials, and the dialogue is:

'And what work of national importance are you doing?'
'Why, I'm rearin' eight children and helping to make airyplanes!'

There were also field service postcards in response to censorship problems. Soldiers were given fawn cards with ready-made statements on them, so that lines could be crossed out, leaving the messages to be delivered. There could be no room for a personal note, and a statement warned the soldier, 'If anything else is added the postcard will be destroyed.' The cards were at first restricted to two cards per man each week. This format of cards was trenchantly utilised by the NCF when they produced their own, to show pictorial images of COs lives and feelings. 'What a CO feels like' for instance, showed a sequence of situations that offered a profile of the various constricted elements of a resister's time in the process of persecution.

The NCF hit back with its own media activities and publications, notably the magazine, *The Tribunal*. The first editor was W. J. Chamberlain, using the National Labour Press, but this was closed down. Scotland Yard were only too happy to close it down when they could. But as the memorial booklet of 1919 recounts, it survived, 'With two skilled comrades, a small hand press bought months before, the paper deposited in various safe quarters, the work went on. Scotland Yard threatened under DORA and other acts. They searched but without avail.' There was constant harassment though. For instance, Joan Beauchamp, whose imprint was on the paper, was arrested and fined, with the threat of imprisonment if not paid. Detectives went on looking for the *Tribunal* but failed.

The tribunals also raised a question relating to another dimension of what was, essentially, a kind of trial. Were the pronouncements made by the panel members privileged – that is, equal to such words spoken in a proper court within the law of the land? The various printings of the Army regulations since 1881 had bundled together 'courts of inquiry, committees and boards' for a variety of uses and cases; but how did they relate to courts per se? Also, could words spoken by panel members be subject to law? The issue came to a head in an action for slander brought against the Revd W. Harvey-Smith who had allegedly 'maliciously spoken and published' words at a Lincolnshire tribunal. He had said that some farmers were involved in 'a big swindle'. The result was that, as Katherine Storr has summarised, 'Tribunals owed their existence to the National Registration Act 1915, Section 2, and the Military Service Act, Schedule 2. His Lordship [Mr Justice Sankey] declared that the tribunal was a judicial body and statements made at sittings were absolutely privileged. Costs were awarded to the plaintiffs, but leave to appeal was granted.' This meant that, for instance, a man sitting on a tribunal panel could pass any kind of opinion on a CO standing before him, and be inviolate.

Situations such as this kept on recurring, as the haphazardly arranged wartime system encountered problems. But as early as the end of February 1916, the press was reporting that the establishment was happy with the standardisation of the system. One report announced, 'Meanwhile delay is being reduced to a minimum in the work of the tribunals; their decisions are gradually approximating to a standardised system and there is an appearance of greater firmness about the proceedings.' This was written on 24 February, and the writer adds, 'No total exemptions were granted in London yesterday. Some applications still seem to be made on trivial grounds.' Rarely was a report on the subject so biased and prejudiced. It is a perfect instance of 'spin'. The tribunals, based on all the evidence we have, were harsh, bigoted and reductive in their decisions and pronouncements. In terms of the war resisters who stood in the dock, their challenge was to find a way to be properly understood by a group of people whose brief was primarily to dismiss claims, under the bullying presence of the military member of their assembly. With hindsight we read with modern eyes and a fuller understanding, accounts in which individuals tried to speak of their moral beliefs and their reasons in refusing to take another life in a hostile setting of pre-judgement and perfunctory expression of opinion. The tribunal reports often read as though the panels had a checklist and that nothing ever veered from the questions and criticism on that list.

In the centre of the conflict, like a beacon of reason, stood the

NCF. Their stance had been made clear very early in that fateful year of 1916, when men were to be forced to be taken to the front and to carry arms. They produced a leaflet headed 'Repeal the Act', and this credo made it clear that the NCF saw the conscription process as a crime. The key statement was this:

Fellow citizens – conscription is now the law in this free country of free traditions. Our hard-won liberties have been violated. Conscription means the desecration of principles that we have long held dear; it involves the subordination of civil liberties to military dictation; it imperils the freedom of individual conscience, and establishes in our midst that militarism which menaces all social progress and divides the people of all nations.

W. J. Chamberlain, in his account of the NCF, notes that 750,000 copies of the leaflet were circulated and that 'when all but a dozen had been distributed, and of the afternoon of 12 March, CID officers arrived at the offices'. It was, again, an instance of DORA in operation.

*

Across the land there were discussions and meetings. Entirely typical was one announced in the local press in Grimsby in January, with the new Act only just presented from the House: 'Conscription: De we need it? A debate on the above subject will take place at the Social Union ... on Saturday 16 January between Mr Bamforth (affirmative) and Mr Sowden (negative). Admission free. Refreshments.'

Yet the tribunals went on, and among thousands of examples that could be outlined, the following may suffice to show one of the most typical situations. This is the case of Percy Rosewarne, who had been too young to fight in the Boer War, but had joined the Green Howards as a band boy under Part VI of the Queen's Regulations, which allowed youngsters to enlist as long as they were 'boys of good character between the ages of 14 and 16 … for the purpose of being trained as trumpeters, drummers, buglers, musicians or tailors'. When the demands of 1914 came he went to enlist in the infantry with two friends, but pulled out when his friends were rejected. Then something happened to change his thinking. Stephen Lewis, writing about the case, suggests it might have been his reading of the moralist and art critic, John Ruskin. Percy was a railwayman, and so initially in a reserved occupation; but after industrial trouble, he was liable to be called up, and so began his new struggle of conscience.

He went through the same ridiculous succession of courts martial as Scott Duckers, but he had some experiences of terrible oppression all his own later when in prison, such as the following, recalled by his son:

> Six warders came in and they asked him three times [if he would put on the uniform] and he refused three times, and so they tied the whole of the uniform and the equipment with flex around his neck and then they threw him up in the air and he hit the ceiling of the cell and crashed to the floor.

It is, then, now an appropriate time to turn the focus onto this prison experience of the resisters.

4

PRISON AND THE HOME OFFICE SCHEME

One of the most informative ways of seeing and understanding the nature of the imprisonment for COs is to survey the various prisons across the country and relate them to the memoirs we have of the CO inmates. Basically, the prison experience of these men was effected at a time when the prison system was little different from the late-Victorian standardisation brought about by Edmund du Cane; that is, a prison was severe, restrictive, ostensibly aiming at a curative or corrective result by means of an imposed regime of restrictions, deprivation and discipline. Just a few years after the war, Fenner Brockway and Stephen Cooper wrote an in-depth analysis, with a thorough documentary aim, on the whole prison system, and in that large volume they included the answers to a questionnaire given to a CO. This is worth some attention, before a survey in this chapter which aims at recounting the biographies of a selection of COs who were incarcerated because of their status as absolutists or because they had been forcibly drafted as soldiers and so received prison sentences for disobedience. Brockway and

Cooper head this 'Evidence of a Political Prisoner' – expressed with the confidence of radicals who had seen the end of the horrendous war to which they had refused to go.

The first port of call for a large number of COs was Wormwood Scrubs. One of the great landmarks of East Acton, this place emerged as the heart of a new prison system. Significantly, in contrast to convict prisons, which were built like castles, with a central tower and radiated wings, this 'local prison' comprised four parallel blocks with a linking corridor. It was further boosted with the addition of a new gatehouse in 1885 and a chapel in 1883, all under the auspices of Director of Convict Prisons Edmund Du Cane.

Writing in 1891, George Millin provided an account for *The Star*, giving a very good impression of the prison as it had developed by then:

> Since 1875, this vast pile, with its one thousand three hundred odd cells, chapel, workshops, kitchens, bath house, and hospital, has been slowly rising and it now seems to be the *ne plus ultra* of the art of sanitary construction. Dismal a place as it necessarily is, Wormwood Scrubs is probably the healthiest abode in the entire kingdom.

Yet it was not all a matter of punishment and repression; from the early years there was a concern for education and rehabilitation. In 1899, the London School Board wrote to the Home Secretary offering to give a course of lectures to the prisoners at the Scrubs. This was welcomed, with a stipulation as to what might be given: 'The Home Secretary added that if the Board were prepared to arrange for a system of lectures to young offenders under 24 on commercial, scientific or other subjects of the kind given by Miss Honnor Morten, he was of the opinion that such an experiment might well be made.' The woman in question was a journalist, educationist and suffragette who had given lessons on hygiene and first aid to the women prisoners in Holloway. As one paper noted of her, 'Thus she was able to break down the prison rule of silence, bringing in a human interest into the women's awful existence.' She died in 1913.

What would be the most typical type of prisoner in the 1890s when everything was running smoothly and all building work was finished? Perhaps it would be someone like Thomas Abberley. His prison profile in the official records includes this information:

Place of birth: London

Place where last offence was committed: London

Date of conviction: 3/12/1888

Prison from which liberated: Wormwood Scrubs

Date of liberation: 3/10/1893

Destination on discharge: Marygold Court, Battersea

Remarks: 7 previous convictions

Thomas was a recidivist, known then as a 'habitual offender'. Note his address on liberation. The only help he could have hoped for, to help him re-settle in society, was a Prisoners' Aid Association or perhaps, if he was still in touch, with a police court missionary. There was no probation service until 1907.

The report of the Prisons Commissioners made in 1902 stated that there had been a huge growth in the statistics of the prison population. The criminal prisons of London for the past decade had shown that, 'The commitments in the metropolis have increased from 38,373 to 53,591.' There was a reshuffle of London prisons in terms of their specific nature and provision; so

Holloway became a prison for women only, and Brixton 'a house of detention for males only'. These changes made Wormwood Scrubs transfer its women prisoners. In 1904, just after the last female prisoners were removed and dispersed, it became a borstal.

*

We have a clear notion of what it was like to serve a stretch in the institution in the early twentieth century, mainly from memoirs. One outstanding example of this is an autobiography written by Arthur Harding. He was born in 'The Nichol' – a very poor area of London – and was inducted into a life of crime in the underworld before being rehabilitated. Harding told his story to the oral historian, Raphael Samuel, and the Harding material is now kept at the Bishopsgate Institute. From his autobiography we learn a great deal about life and conditions at the prison in the late nineteenth century. He gives a vivid documentary account: 'The first thing I noticed in the cell was that I had no bed to sleep on. Some eminent Christian with the love of Christ in his heart had ordained hard work, the treadmill, hard fare, gruel and dried bread, hard board, and a plank of wood to sleep on.'

Harding gave a very powerful version of those images of prison life which are universal, the expressions of pain and anguish as a result of isolation, extreme frustration and mental strain; as in one memory of a fracas in the night: 'His ravings and screams are very disturbing to the other inmates and can be heard all over the hall. The night patrol summons assistance and a number of warders arrive to take the poor, demented creature to the padded cells.'

The harsh conditions he describes in terms of the treadwheel and the physical labour and the plank for a bed obtained before *c*. 1900. But certainly for the first thirty years of its existence,

Wormwood Scrubs would have had the old features of the jails as they were first created around 1820. At the heart of the regime was the aforementioned treadwheel. This had been invented by William Cubitt in 1816, and fitted the new penitentiary ideal perfectly. The Select Committee on Penitentiary Houses of 1810–11 had recommended that the government take over the task of making a national penitentiary at Millbank in London – the wheel was central to this regime.

The COs in 1916 were to mix with a few celebrities – a feature that has always been marked in the history of the Scrubs. One of the earliest celebrities to spend a little time inside the walls was Dr Jameson. *The Illustrated London News* carried a sketch of a scene at Bow Street in 1896 with the heading, 'The Penalty of Non-Success' and the note: 'Dr Jameson and his officers, charged with unlawfully fitting out a military expedition against a friendly state, to wit, the South African Republic.' 'Dr Jim' as he was called by some reporters, was guilty, and was taken to the Scrubs.

What he and his small army of 800 men had done, as part of a conspiracy led by Cecil Rhodes, was to lead a force of cavalry into the Transvaal. The romp was a failure, and of course, this was a serious crime. Jameson, whose first names were Leander Starr, made an impact on the popular imagination and stirred up debate and disagreement. In fact, the jury reported that they could not agree on a verdict, but the Lord Chief Justice, as one report has it, told the jury that they had de facto brought in a verdict of guilty. The foreman then stood up and said that yes, they were all agreed on guilty.

Jameson was given fifteen months; what is especially interesting is his treatment when he arrived at the Scrubs: 'Every indignity was spared them that could be dispensed with. After the usual formalities before the Governor and head warder, they were taken to the bathroom ... Dr Jameson and his companions were then passed on to Dr Pasmore, the medical officer ... Dr Jameson and Dr Patmore had both graduated from the same college in 1877.'

They were well looked after. At six they were given porridge and bread, and they were given ground floor cells, with plenty of light and air. There was no hard plank for their beds, but they were given mattresses and pillows. In fact, they were segregated from common criminals. This gives a rare insight into the treatment of political prisoners as opposed to the everyday rogues. For breakfast the next day they were even given a pint of cocoa and some bread – and the much denigrated 'skilly' was spared them. This was the thin gruel, also known as 'stirabout'. They were soon transferred elsewhere.

The other top-class celebrity villain who entered a cell in the Scrubs in the early decades was the infamous fraudster, Jabez Balfour. Here was a man who had lied and embezzled his way to wealth and then run off to South America with young women, eventually to be tracked down by a determined sleuth. His destiny was to spend nine years behind bars; he started the sentence at the Scrubs. As his biographer, David McKie points out, Balfour did not look at himself in the mirror for the whole of his sentence, and his remarks on finally gazing at the man he saw say a lot about how a stretch in a Victorian jail does plenty of damage: 'I shall never forget the shock. I started from it with affright, for I can honestly affirm that I did not recognize a single feature of the face that I beheld reflected in it ... I learnt then for the first time the full and sorrowful significance of the tears which I had seen in the eyes of the two or three relatives and dear friends who had visited me in my bonds.' He had gone from a stocky gentleman in an expensive suit and top hat to prisoner number V460.

The COs were to find the Scrubs quite a manageable place – when compared with their usual second location, at a convict prison such as Dartmoor.

*

The questions in the survey concern the prison regime. They focus on care, health, cleanliness and communications, in the main. Somewhat surprisingly, the responses were not as severe and critical as might have been expected. For instance, one area of real importance for articulate, educated men such as the COs, was books and writing:

> *What were the arrangements for reading? Remark on these.*
> Answer: Prison libraries vary ... was shocking ... seemed fairly good ... At my first sentence at — there was no chance of seeing a catalogue or choosing books at all, and we had to take whatever rubbish was given us. I got two really good books during the 112 days. Evenings were allowed for reading in most prisons, though we were supposed to work until ...
> *What facilities were allowed for writing?*
> Answer: One slate in most prisons. I managed to get two at — . Letters according to prison rules. No other facilities at all. I would suggest that prisoners be allowed to use notebooks. If any danger of being wrongly used for illicit correspondence, a system of numbered pages, to be examined each week by landing officer could easily be devised.

Other negative comments were that it was futile trying to complain to visiting magistrates, approach the governor, get proper medical attention, rely on every warder to be helpful, or express real criticism. The most heartfelt comments concerned ill treatment; one CO answered: 'In many cases the physical effects of imprisonment were most marked. Men became thin and haggard. Many were mentally affected. I fancy that after the first month's solitary confinement most men are in a very plastic condition and might be influenced for good at that period. After that, a sort of dullness seems to settle on them.'

*

The Welsh experience of CO punishment is a rich source in the history of pacifism. Much of this links to HMP Wormwood Scrubs.

To be a CO in 1916 was to strive against a current as strong as the mightiest river: the Reverend Harding Rees, for instance, brought up in Llangennech, was destined to be sent to a work camp in Ireland, and of all the voices in the First World War, he recognised the nature of what was really opposing him. He wrote after seeing trees felled in great numbers, and seeing there a metaphor of loss and death, 'All this insatiable rapacity was the result of war which can only leave a blight on all things and a curse.'

Were the COs cowards or were they brave heroes for peace? The majority of people in 1916 knew exactly where they stood on that issue. But today? The jury may always be on the efficacy of such pacifism, but there is no doubting the courage of the people who kept to their values: from intellectuals such as T. H. Parry-Williams and T. Gwynn Jones to long-term prisoner George Maitland Davies, they proved the maxim that 'the unexamined life is not worth living' and Milton's famous lines, 'Peace hath her victories/ No less renowned than war.'

At the very heart of the conscription regime was a Welshman, the most famous of his day, David Lloyd George. He had found it essential to back the conscription drive out of sheer necessity and his allegiance to the dominant establishment ideology around him. In Wales there was a high proportion of COs, around one thousand from the British total of 16,500, but 280,000 Welshmen served in the war years as historians have often pointed out.

The Scrubs had its fair share of 'conchie' prisoners in the First World War, and another Welshman is arguably one of the most significant prisoners in this group: Thomas Jones, later to be made Baron Maelor. Jones was born in 1898 near Wrexham, and he started out in life as a miner, at Bersham Colliery. Moving on to acquire an education, he studied at Normal College, Bangor, before becoming a teacher.

Along with so many others of his countrymen, he refused to carry a gun against the Kaiser in 1914, and after agreeing to have a non-combatant role, he still found that obeying orders was a problem and was given a six-month sentence. So began his time in the Scrubs, before being transferred to Dartmoor for some hard labour. The context behind this sentence (and the original offence) is that the Army made it very tough for conscientious objectors who had taken up non-combatant roles. Research, based mainly on oral history and a few records, has shown that as well as brutal field punishments, such men as Jones were easily exposed to a range of vicious punitive regimes in the Army.

Jones was court-martialled before being sent to jail; he was confirmed as a socialist, and returned to civilian life eager to make a mark politically. He was a member of the Independent Labour Party in 1919, and in the 1930s he contested Merioneth. In 1951 he won the seat, and carried on as an MP until his retirement in 1966. He died in 1984.

Historian Geraint Jenkins has given some vivid examples of the suffering Welsh COs at the time:

Ithel Davies, a farm labourer from Montgomeryshire, was placed in a straitjacket while in custody, and was badly beaten by prison officers. George Maitland Lloyd Davies, a former soldier, was locked up in four different prisons, and literally refashioned the sword given to him as an officer with the Royal Welsh Fusiliers into a sickle, which he displayed in his office at the Fellowship of Reconciliation in London.

One of the most illustrious Welsh prisoners at this time was the poet Gwenallt, real name David James Jones, born in 1899. He later became a major figure in modern Welsh literature. He is known by the bardic name of Gwenallt, which is a reversal of Alltwen, the village close to his place of birth in Pontardawe. He was conscripted in 1917, and after facing a tribunal as a CO, he was sent to the Scrubs like the future Baron Maelor, and then on to Dartmoor. Gwenallt was later to become a founding member of the Welsh Academy, and a member of Plaid Cymru.

Recent research into other First World War COs has brought to light a man who shared a cell with Gwenallt: Thomas Rhys Davies. His family historian points out that Davies, like many Welsh nationalists at the time, looked across the sea to Ireland, and to events in Dublin. The rebellion of Easter 1916 happened just as the tribunals of the Military Service Act were in full swing in England. Gwenallt's writing was inspired by the cultural life he saw in Irish-speaking Ireland. Obviously, he and Davies shared common opinions regarding this nascent nationalism; but Thomas Davies somehow managed to be transferred from the

Scrubs to a work allocation back home on the Carmarthenshire farm.

As for Gwenallt, he later published widely and to great acclaim, mainly in fiction and poetry; his collected works were published in 2001 – *Cerddi Gwenallt*, from the Gomer press.

Other Welsh COs left accounts of their time in the Scrubs, one of the most telling being that of Mansel Grenfell, who shared his time inside with Dan Harvey and Morgan Jones. One writer notes, 'The only chance of communication was in the prison chapel when they spoke in Welsh as the others sang the refrains of hymns.'

As a dark footnote to the treatment of COs in prisons, it has to be pointed out that there were work camps dotted around the land – three in Wales – in which there were evidently some very rough and brutal punishments applied to men who would not fight the Germans. Compared to the destinies of those inmates, the regime at Wormwood Scrubs was a rather more accommodating option. But this secret history is only hinted at in obscure publications or through the stories of the effects on their families, where this is available. One example of the forgotten and unrecorded history of this subject is Red Roses camp, in Carmarthenshire. This later became a holiday camp after the Second World War, but at the time of the First World War it was the destination of 'conchies' – and the regime ground these men down. For instance, Andrew Peddieson of Glasgow died while interned at the camp, ostensibly of flu 'under terrible conditions of crowding and neglect', according to a writer in the 1920s. He had tried his best to nurse other victims in that massive flu epidemic, 'in spite of the Agent's obstructions and insults. Till he collapsed himself.'

*

As well as looking at some representative prison experiences of COs, it is useful to have an account of the British prison system as it was at the time of the war.

It is something of a paradox that it was Disraeli's Conservatives who passed the 1877 Prisons Act and brought about centralisation. Such policies were not entrenched in their manifesto, but it was an age of pragmatism in politics and all the sensible arguments were applied in the debate. It was the Home Secretary, Assheton Cross, who introduced the bill for its first reading. His main contentions were that the prisons were expensive to manage and that the system was outdated, with too many small prisons on the list in the provinces. Behind the move was a basic political policy: the Conservatives had promised to reduce local rates, and taking the prisons into centralisation was one way to do that.

Cross made an influential speech, with issues of waste and poor management being addressed along with a critique of the state of the prisons. There were opponents, of course; the main argument being the same one that had been applied when other services were centralised – factories, education and so on. The voices against the move said that there would be incompetence, huge rises in running costs and that it was just not right to interfere with the principal of local government.

But the thought that at last a great deal of power would be taken from local magistrates pleased many; they were totally autonomous, thus leaving their powers open to abuse. The Act would place the Home Secretary in control. There were fresh objections from the provinces: a petition from Nottingham was presented, and Oxford City Council complained, stating that they had only recently spent a very large sum of money on their establishment, and if it were to change then that would have been wasted. But after a debate on 12 July, the bill became law.

The Secretary of State was now the person in command of the prison service. It was he who would appoint staff and he who would have the powers previously in the hands of the justices, those powers applied to acts, common law and charters. Justices in their normal work were no longer to have any direct influence on prisons; visiting justices were to be in place, something that prefigured the later boards of visitors.

The new organisation at the centre was the Prison Commission, with five commissioners. The new body would have to make reports to parliament and appoint senior staff across the country. The first commissioner was, of course, Sir Edmund Du Cane. It has been said about the man that he could boast that he could look at his watch at any time of the day and know exactly what any one of the prisoners in England would be doing. Du Cane was a product of the Royal Military Academy at Woolwich; he became a lieutenant in the Royal Engineers when he was only eighteen, and retired with the rank of major general in 1887. He had worked in convict prisons in Western Australia, and his interest in the prison system grew partly with his friendship with Sir Edward Henderson, Chief Commissioner of the Metropolitan Police. In 1863 he was appointed as Director of Convict Prisons and Inspector of Military Prisons. He was knighted in 1877 when he took the job as commissioner in the new prison system.

Du Cane held the belief that a criminal tendency is the basis of all mankind, and saw 'career criminals' as fools who were too weak ever to look into themselves and change; hence he rejected the religion-based attitudes of previous years. The task ahead in

1877 was to make prisons cost-effective, and places so formidable that they would be a deterrent to would-be offenders. He came up with a four-stage regime for the prisoner:

Stage 1: Nine months held in absolute separation, and with 6–10 hours of hard labour each day. Prisoner had no mattress for the first two weeks of the sentence and was allowed only religious books.

Stage 2: The work became less severe; prisoner was allowed limited association and one library book per week.

Stage 3: A small release gratuity was in place and more books available.

Stage 4: Prisoner was now eligible for special employment and the release gratuity was raised.

As with all cost-cutting enterprises, places and people were dispensed with across the land; by the time of Du Cane's retirement in 1895, the number of local prisons had been reduced from 113 to 59.

In order to assess the state of things during this period, before the arrival of the borstal system in 1908, we are fortunate in having an account of a local prison, Northallerton, written by R. G. Alford, a civil engineer, who visited the prison in 1904. A full summary of this description is included as appendix 2 in the present work, but his account does give the modern reader some idea of the space, light and possible movement inside the prison at the time. For example, he noted that A Wing was the best part of the prison as it had six roof lights along the corridor and was

paved with York stone. He measured a typical cell on that wing –
A126 – and made these remarks:

> Measured six feet two by thirteen feet by eight feet ten inches high,
> with arched roof, window three feet six by one foot six, rectangular,
> in fourteen panes, one of perforated zinc. Lock with bevelled bolt. A
> good staircase at each end of the corridor. There are water closets on
> West side only, in centre, but to each flat. There are 114 cell spaces
> in this wing.

He noted that there were 191 men in the gaol and no women –
the reception of women prisoners had ceased in 1904, just before
his second visit there. Health matters were clearly considerably
improved since the days of regular diarrhoea and dysentery; Alford
reports that in the hospital, placed over the men's reception area,
there were two wards, each with four beds, and only one bed was
occupied when he visited. His note about the walls conjures up
the stereotype of every hospital wall from *Carry On* films to early
national health establishments: 'The walls were all coloured in
green 'Duresco.' (That was clearly a patent hard-wearing paint,
matte and dull.)

What had formerly been the women's area in the prison was,
he noted, 'decidedly dark, having but 6 end windows to the east
in gable, and a stair at the other, or inner, end.' Occupations were
hinted at in his list of buildings: kitchen, artisans' shop, wheel
house, industrial shop, crank house (still in use), photo house
and clothes store (the last two as separate buildings inside the
south-east corner). Notably absent were the treadmills, which had
been abolished in 1898. Northallerton has the dubious distinction
of being one of the last few places to still have a crank house as

late as 1904; there were only five left across the country in 1901, so Alford's little note in 1904 that the crank house was 'still in use' hints at a special feature of Northallerton, though not one to brag about. It may well have been the last prison to use a crank house as a punishment.

Du Cane wrote a book explaining his principles, *Account of Penal Servitude in England*, in which he argued that the years from around 1858–72 presented an opportunity for new experiments in penology; the second edition of his book, in 1895, brought about an appraisal in a *Times* leader in which they examined the statistical results. Serious crime was diminishing and short-sentence imprisonment figures had declined, but the comparative numbers in penal servitude in the years 1871 and 1882 remained very much the same. The debate centred on the principles recounted in the newspaper:

> The approved objects of punishment are deterrent and reformatory; to deter the offender himself from repeating his offence and others from imitating it, and to effect an amelioration in his character and habits. How the Directors of Convict Prisons pursue these ends in their management is an old tale.

The writer goes on to affirm the benefits of the new system in terms of work achieved and skills acquired: 'Out of 9,107 prisoners in custody on 1 July 1882, 3,235 acquired their craft in the prison.' Finally, the leader also points out that one prominent reform since 1878 was 'the separation of the worst criminals from the rest; and in 1879–80 another important step was taken in the same direction – the formation of a class of prisoners inexperienced in crime.'

That essay had summarised the central issues in the historical prison system: contamination, inmates forming interior hierarchies and the need to exert management by a minority authority. The secret of Du Cane's success was militarism: the few could organise and manage the many by means of the right structure and the right discipline. The ideal new staff organisation was one governor, one chief warder, four principal warders, eight warders and sixteen assistant warders. This was the case in Reading or Wandsworth, for instance. Underpinning all this was the establishment of salaried staff and of the end of local nepotism. Before centralisation there had been local abuses, such as the following, a very typical situation described by the Governor of Pentonville:

> I can tell you a tale of the old days when a particular prison governorship was considered the plum of the service, and half a dozen governors were selected after careful enquiry by the Visiting Justices; but when the matter came before Quarter Sessions a gentleman, who had nothing to do with the running of the prison before that, whipped up the whole of the county magistrates, and they put the whole of the six governors on one side and selected him as governor.

In other words, the new attitudes and organisation was meant to cure all kinds of evils in the local implementations of the criminal justice system.

In his farewell letter to his prison colleagues, Du Cane wrote, in *The Times* of 1895:

> I trust and believe that this change [prison centralisation] has been not only to the advantage of the public, but to the officers of the

enlarged Department, and I am glad to take this opportunity of acknowledging how much its successful accomplishment has been due to the loyal and intelligent co-operation of those whose aid was necessary to bring it into effect.

The Rosebery Committee, meeting in 1883, made it possible for prison staff to complain. As the prison service was modelled on the Army structure, complaint was for many years out of the question. But in the same years in which the first agitation for police service reform began, the prison officers were also caught up in movements for proper professional conditions and terms of employment.

Then, in 1891, the de Ramsey Report looked at their conditions of service; officers in both local and convict prisons had put in requests for consideration of an increase in pay, a change in promotion procedure, an increase in annual leave, a reduction in working hours and more superannuation on the annual scale. Local staff were given a pay award, free quarters and an allowance for boots. Chief warders had a considerable increase in pay. The notion of overtime was introduced after that report also; it was a reasonable compromise for the local men. As for convict prison workers, they were not so lucky; they had no pay increase. It seemed to be a petty affair, with even a proposal for the deduction of sick leave from annual leave.

Against this background, with the prison routines settled well into the regulations established by the 1877 Act, the COs arrived. Whereas for normal, criminal prisoners there was the set sentence plan of some kind of progression towards reform or at least useful occupation, for the war resisters, the stress was on deprivation and punishment. In many ways this was a return to the punitive, dead-end ways of the houses of correction in the first decades of the nineteenth century, previous to recent reforms.

We have an abundance of prison memoirs from the COs, but the settings for the following tales spans the civil prisons, the military prisons and then the work camps established after the Home Office Scheme. The latter will be explained later in this chapter.

*

The chronicle of the prison experience must begin with the astounding fact that sixty-nine COs died after arrest, and ten while in prison. The dead men were: Walter None of Birkenhead, O. S. Bridle of Brighton, E. Burns of Failsworth, A. Butler of Stockport, P. Campbell of the Isle of Skye, P. L. Gillan of London, A. Horton of Manchester, F. Wilkinson of Dulwich, A. Wilson of Blackburn and J. G. Winter of Cornsay.

In July 1917, Corder Catchpool, a CO prisoner who wrote a memoir of his time inside, compiled some lists of COs in prison. He wrote that 710 men were locked up who had either refused to appear before the central tribunal, or refused the Home Office Scheme. He managed to obtain statistics on the numbers of men inside, including which prisons they were kept at at that time. Wandsworth led the way, with 111 men, followed by Winchester with 88 and Exeter with 49. He also logged the religious classifications of 307 men – these ranged from 109 Quakers to 5 spiritualists and 5 Theosophists.

Bearing in mind the survey of the situation in British prisons as they were in 1914 presented above, the memoirs and evidence we have of prison life for the CO provides a parallel pattern of experience. Corder Catchpool, who was in Ipswich prison for a long stretch, explains this in his book, *Letters of a Prisoner.* Scott Duckers, previously discussed, also offers a detailed account of privations suffered inside the walls; and we further know from the Richmond prisoners what conditions were like.The CO was considered by the prison regime as something quite different from the ordinary criminal. The CO may have thought of himself as a political prisoner, equal to the Sinn Feiners who were kept at Fron Goch camp after the 1916 Easter Rising, but in effect within the prisons he was seen as simply a weak coward who deserved to suffer; he was regularly compared with 'our boys out at the front' and all they had to endure. Prison, for the CO, had practically no approach or aim other than retribution. The mindset was, if you will not kill Germans and put your life on the line for your country, then you are lower than the enemy.

The ingredients of their prison life were hard physical work, little association time, starvation diets, harsh punishment, very little cultural and educational enrichment, tough censorship and restrictions of movement. They were isolated in a variety of ways, and so there developed a strong reliance on pastoral visits, lobbying from outside for alleviation of conditions, as well as the usual small comforts wherever they could be supplied.

Catchpool's deprivation may be seen in the matter of his teeth. For months his teeth gave him pain, and in his letters home he gives the facts: 'I am sorry I cannot give quite so good a report of myself as usual. The continued nagging of petty tooth trouble, coupled with a good deal of sleeplessness, has caused some wear and tear.' This was followed with a report on the problem three weeks later, 'I had heard on the previous Monday that my Home Office petition to see a dentist had been granted.' Then at last he has some treatment: 'The surgery is the most elaborate one I have ever been in ... of course my teeth have been allowed to go far too long unattended, and so give much more trouble than there need have been.'

Catchpool, in contrast to what seems a secondary concern, does give one of the most vivid pictures of the kinds of privations the COs had:

> Between the patient schooling of one's whole being to face the prospect of prolonged imprisonment ... I am compelled to admit that the war may go on for many years ... between the prospect of that wild impetus, if only in imagination, to fervent activity, lies a gulf so great that in respect of its uncertainty at least, life at present may perhaps be claimed to be true campaigning.

One part of this penal regime offered some kind of help – the work of the Quaker chaplains. In 1919, Henry Harris, one such visitor, wrote an account of what he was there for: 'The Quaker chaplain set out to bring some degree of spirituality to the men in prison. Look at his position how you will, that was his work, that was the sole justification of his appointment.' He raised a question to answer – what was he to teach? He saw the work as being like that of 'the pupil and the flock'. He concluded, 'If we were not fully fitted for the work of a pastor when we began our ministry inside the prisons, we were surely abundantly better fitted for pastoral work outside, after a few months of work within.'

Yet, in spite of attempts to look for beams of light and hope in this context, the hard fact remains that an unacceptable number of deaths occurred in custody. In the first full history of the Fellowship, the list of deaths in custody includes minimal details of the list of men and their home towns. Some, however, are extremely poignant, such as the note about Moss – Morley, 'Died in York Military Hospital. Further particulars refused.'

*

From the summer of 1916 the necessity of having some kind of alternative service for the absolutists in prison became too urgent to ignore. What emerged came to be known as the Home Office Scheme. This directive has been linked to the notion of one of British history's most egregious euphemisms – the 'settlement' – and also by extension to T. H. W. Pelham, who was the chairman of the committee responsible for this huge failure. The basic assignment, the brief for Pelham's men, was announced in March. *The Times* had it in a nutshell: 'It is announced by the Board of Trade that the government have appointed a committee to which a tribunal may refer for advice as to what service of national importance an applicant for exemption on the grounds of conscientious objection should undertake.' On the surface, that seems very worthy and admirable. But the outcome was to be disastrous, replacing prison with something not far removed from a hybrid that mixed boot camp with convict outpost. The problem facing the government was that the failure of the tribunals to deal with those applicants whose beliefs were found to be genuine posed all kinds of difficulties.

As J. Morgan Jones pointed out in 1919, there were two categories of men who were eligible for the work in what became known as settlements, 'Those religious objectors who were always willing to do work of national importance but had not been recognised by a tribunal' and the 'Socialist or moral objectors who would not submit to military discipline.'

John Graham, in his 1919 history, gives a full account of the

Home Office Scheme. He noted that Lloyd George, who was then Prime Minister leading a coalition, had no time at all for the absolutists and wanted to make their path 'as hard as possible'. But against these extremist views there were the powerful intellects who bolstered the resisters' cause, such as Bertrand Russell, who, in the fundamental debate on what work the prisoners should do, asked Lloyd George, 'Would he himself have been willing to spend all his time during the Boer War in growing cabbages?'

Decisions were made; the genuine COs, it was pronounced, would be released from civil prison on their undertaking to perform work of national importance under civil control. After Pelham's first involvement there came William Brace, Under-Secretary at the Home Office, who had to finalise the details.

Clifford Allen of the NCF soon declaimed the shortcomings of the scheme, which was ostensibly a promise to provide meaningful and relevant work to the prisoners, rather than shut them up in gaol. Allen's main criticisms were that there would be no diligence or due process regarding individuals; indeed, there were no tribunal proceeding records to consult, and there would only be further severe penalties imposed on those who were not considered to be 'genuine' in the account given of their conscientious objection to enlistment.

This led to a letter written to Asquith by the NCF National Committee insisting that the scheme operate with the proviso that 'it is of the first importance that men who feel called upon to accept work under civil control should be satisfied that they are rendering service of real value to the community.' The letter added, 'The conditions should be that men should be set to the work for which they have skill ... they should not be set tasks connected with the organisation of war, or which would liberate other men,

SHORT SERVICE.

(For the Duration of the War, with the Colours and in the Army Reserve).

Card No. [ ]

ATTESTATION OF

No. *133446* Name *Wybert Butle* Corps *ROYAL GARR. ARTY.*

Questions to be put to the Recruit before Enlistment.

1. What is your Name?	1.	*Wybert Butle*
2. What is your full Address?	2.	*4 Tatt.... Street Middlesbrough*
3. Are you a British Subject?	3.	*Yes*
4. What is your Age?	4.	*33* Years ... Months
5. What is your Trade or Calling?	5.	*Insurance Agent*
6. Are you Married?	6.	*Yes*
7. Have you ever served in any branch of His Majesty's Forces, naval or military, if so*, which?		*No*
8. Are you willing to be vaccinated or re-vaccinated?		*Yes*
9. Are you willing to be enlisted for General Service?	9.	*Yes*
10. Did you receive a Notice, and do you understand its meaning, and who gave it to you?	10.	*Yes* { Name *H. J. Horne* Corps *R.G.A.*

11. Are you willing to serve upon the following conditions provided His Majesty should so long require your services?

For the duration of the War, at the end of which you will be discharged with all convenient speed. You will be required to serve for one day with the Colours and the remainder of the period in the Army Reserve, in accordance with the provisions of the Royal Warrant dated 20th Oct., 1915, until such time as you may be called up by order of the Army Council. If employed with Hospitals, depots of Mounted Units, or as a Clerk, etc., you may be retained after the termination of hostilities until your services can be spared, but such retention shall in no case exceed six months.

11. ... *Yes*

I, *Wybert Butle* do solemnly declare that the above answers made by me to the above questions are true, and that I am willing to fulfil the engagements made.

Wybert Butle SIGNATURE OF RECRUIT.

Witness Signature of Witness.

OATH TO BE TAKEN BY RECRUIT ON ATTESTATION.

I, *Wybert Butle* swear by Almighty God, that I will be faithful and bear true Allegiance to His Majesty King George the Fifth, His Heirs, and Successors, and that I will, as in duty bound, honestly and faithfully defend His Majesty, His Heirs, and Successors, in Person, Crown, and Dignity against all enemies, and will observe and obey all orders of His Majesty, His Heirs and Successors, and of the Generals and Officers set over me. So help me God.

CERTIFICATE OF MAGISTRATE OR ATTESTING OFFICER.

The Recruit above named was cautioned by me that if he made any false answer to any of the above questions he would be liable to be punished as provided in the Army Act.

The above questions were then read to the Recruit in my presence.

I have taken care that he understands each question, and that his answer to each question has been duly entered as replied to, and the said Recruit has made and signed the declaration and taken the oath before me at *Middlesbrough* on this *1st* day of *December* 191*5*

Signature of the Justice

Certificate of Approving Officer.

I certify that this Attestation of the above-named Recruit is correct, and properly filled up, that the required forms appear to have been complied with. I accordingly approve, and appoint him to the *ROYAL GARR. ARTY*

If enlisted by special authority, Army Form B. 203 (or other authority for the enlistment) will be attached to the original attestation.

Date *18 DEC 1916* 19

Place **SOUTH CAMP, RIPON**

Woolmer MAJOR. R.G.A
COMMDG 4 DEPOT R.G.A } Approving Officer.

† The signature of the Approving Officer is to be affixed in the presence of the Recruit.
‡ Here insert the "Corps" for which the Recruit has been enlisted.

* If so, the Recruit is to be asked the particulars of his former service, and to produce, if possible, his Certificate of Discharge and Certificate of Character, which should be returned to him conspicuously endorsed in red ink, as follows viz:—(Name) re-enlisted in the (Regiment)

Previous page: 1.
A short-service
attestation form for
one Private Birtie.
This tied the potential
recruit to enlistment
when the demand
came. (Courtesy of
Martin Birtle)

Left: 2. The so-called
'insanity box' at
Dartmoor, from
the personal photo
collection of Percy
Smith. (Author's
collection)

Below: 3. A view of
the workshop at the
Knutsford Workshop
Centre, taken by Percy
Smith and kept in
his own unpublished
folder of pictures.
(Author's collection)

Right: 4. Clifford Allen, NCF chairman. He was the driving force behind the organisation and activities of the Fellowship. From NCF Memorial Booklet, 1919. (Author's collection)

Below: 5. Brockway and friends at the time of their trial. The four on the front row, from left to right: Walter Ayles, Chamberlain, Allen and Brockway. From *The No Conscription Fellowship* booklet, 1919. (Author's collection)

Top: 6. Two sketches of prison cells by E. M. Wilson. There was an abundance of creative talent in the CO prisoners, and the executive used these skills wherever possible. The artwork was always a part of the NCF publications. From NCF Memorial Booklet, 1919. (Author's collection)

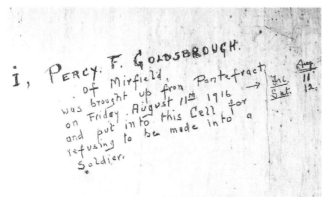

Middle: 7. An example of prison graffiti from Richmond Castle. Many of these men were to become those sentenced to death at Boulogne. (Author's collection)

THE ALTERNATIVE.

Better barren women than children bred for war,
Better death in birth than manhood trained for murder ;
Better bleak wild country than shattered flesh and bone ;
Better voided earth before Primeval Sundawn ;
And better dead blank world if battles still must rage—
        But best of all no war at all,
        And Peace in a Golden Age.

C. G. C.

Bottom: 8. A CO cartoon sympathetic to the cause. (Author's collection)

Above left: 9. Satirical cartoons on the CO life. Humour, as so often in harsh experience, makes the point very forcefully. (Author's collection)

Above right: 10. A popular postcard showing the common view of the weak and effeminate CO. (Author's collection)

Right: 11. Sketches of prison scenes. Another image from an anonymous CO artist from inside the walls. (Author's collection)

MISFITS IN UNIFORM

WHAT'S HAPPENING OUTSIDE?

A VISIT

CAN I STICK IT?

No. L............................ 18 May 19 22

NO MORE WAR MOVEMENT

11 DOUGHTY STREET, W.C.1   'Phone : Museum 9311

Chairman :   General Secretary :   Financial Secretary . WALTER H. AYLES.

A. FENNER BROCKWAY   LUCY A. COX.   Treasurer : HAROLD J. MORLAND.

Received from..........Mr Percy Smith............................

................................Pounds.....Three.....Shillings...........Six.....Pence

Financial Secretary............................ With thanks

£   — : 3 : 6

Above: 12. A receipt for subscription to the No More War campaign. (Author's collection)

Below: 13. A distant view of Dartmoor convict prison. Dartmoor was the prison which offered perhaps more danger to life from outside in the wild than inside doing hard labour. (Author's collection)

Above: 14. A drawing of a prison Quaker meeting, from Corder Catchpool's *Letters from a Prisoner*, 1941. (Author's collection)

Below: 15. Friends' Ambulance Unit workers delivering bread. (Courtesy of Religious Society of Friends [Quakers] in Britain)

H. M. Prison *W. Scrubs*

3 - 2 - 196 7.

Dear *Mother*

I am now in this Prison, and am in *usual* *health*

If I behave well, I shall be allowed to write ~~another~~ letter about

8 weeks time and to receive a reply, but no reply is

allowed to this. *My Sentence is 112 Days*

Signature *T Corder Pettijon Catchpool*

Register No. *2924*

NOTICE OF INCARCERATION

Above: 16. A pro-forma letter home from Corder Catchpool. Catchpool wrote a full account of his time behind bars, and became well known as a disseminator of the more documentary element in CO media work. From *A CO in Prison*, 1916.

Right: 17. Sentenced to death. (Author's collection)

THE MEN SENTENCED TO DEATH

By HUBERT W. PEET

HUBERT W. PEET

(Organising Secretary of the Friends' Service Committee)

THE sudden transference of C.O.s to France in May, 1916, marked the crest of the wave in the efforts of the military authorities to "break" the movement. Riding rough-shod over the promises of the highest civil authorities that objectors would not be taken out of the country, they transferred to France from Landguard Fort, Harwich, from Richmond, Yorks., and from Seaford thirty-seven men, thirty of whom received the death sentence.

The first rumours of the intended move came from Harwich, where the Eastern N.C.C. was stationed and where a party of the earliest arrested C.O.s was in irons at Landguard Fort. A Quaker Chaplain was hurried down as soon as possible, but before his wire was delivered saying that the men were gone, information was received that the N.C.C. and its C.O. prisoners were on their way to Southampton. This warning was conveyed by a letter thrown out of the train by one of the ordinary N.C.C. men while passing through a London suburb.

Efforts were promptly made to reach the party at Southampton, where they were delayed by the discovery of an outbreak of measles in the corps; but before this could be accomplished and before personal representations to Mr. Asquith led to the sending of a telegram ordering their retention in this country, the hitherto exempted ... allowances to dependents should be equal to those granted to soldiers' families.'

There had been a government policy in Wormwood Scrubs, as so many COs had initially been placed there, to 'weed out' absolutists who could be forcibly removed to the Army Reserve at Section W – a move that would have meant that they were, in fact, doing no such kind of military support work. That was not exactly anathema to the individuals concerned, of course. The process was swift and methodical: Lord Salisbury fronted a central tribunal, a panel assigned to assess the prisoners individually; but this was in truth merely a ploy to give the men the same kind of penal future that would have been known as hard labour in any ordinary convict prison. A man who accepted the removal from prison to Section W agreed to 'reside at such a place as the Committee, their agents or representatives may from time to time determine', and he had to 'conform to such regulations as the Committee may lay down for the due execution of the work allotted to him.'

The enterprise was, in fact, applied as a huge exercise in 'doublethink' and patrician euphemism. In effect, a gulag system was in the process of being created under the guise of supposedly productive civilian work, geared to the skills and background of the men.

*

Then arrived the establishment of the camps, or 'settlements' as the jargon had it. Having been deemed to be genuine war resisters 250 men were sent to Aberdeen. Their destiny lay in working the granite quarries, extracting stone for use in road-making.

What sort of iniquities and abuses followed may be gleaned from a letter written to the *Aberdeen Daily Journal* on 12 September

1916 by the men. There were 200 in the camp there, at Dyce, and the letter was written after a death:

Sir,

We, the Men's Committee of the Dyce Camp, have come to the following conclusions concerning the death in this camp of Mr W. L. Roberts, of Stockport, which occurred on Friday, 8 September last: We view the present position as extremely serious and assert that but for indifference and neglect, our late comrade Roberts would be alive now. His death can be traced to the following main causes: men have been sent direct from prisons, hundreds of miles, into exposed and harsh conditions of life. The camp was not in readiness to receive the men sent as regards ordinary feeding arrangements, the provision of nursing facilities, including suitable feeding and housing of sick, etc. The medical attention is inadequate. The recommendations of the Men's Committee re accommodation, clothing and general conditions were largely ignored. Up to the time of our late comrade's decease, there appeared to be no proper appreciation of the position by those responsible, and the urgency of adequate improvements in the conditions obtaining in the camp.

The circumstances of this letter of protest were that men who were already considerably weakened after long stretches in prison were given the toughest variety of hard labour. The men behind the letter had wet tents for their homes, the road officials in the local area were in charge and a shift system was used. The work began to take its toll. As Graham, the historian of the NCF wrote, 'The local doctor certified many men as physically unfit for work.' The one brief respite was that they could go to the Quakers' meeting house at weekends and have tea and talk.

Something should have been learned from the bad experience at Dyce, which was closed in October. But the settlements were being opened all across the land. Old prisons were adapted for this use, such as at Wakefield, formerly a house of correction in the sixteenth century. It was such an ancient place that Yorkshire residents had the phrase 'sent to Wakefield' as an equivalent to 'being given a prison sentence' in their regional parlance. This was now changed for the COs. Graham wrote that there were 600 men stationed there, with the warders changed into 'instructors'. Locks were removed, and the place was converted into a massive workshop, in effect. The same process was duly followed for other places; but at Wakefield, something happened that highlighted some of the inherent problems of the scheme. A planned riot occurred, with goods robbed, windows broken and furniture damaged. The whole enterprise was under stress and seemed doomed. By the end of 1916, as Graham notes, 'a small group, including Cornelius Barritt, H. E. Stanton and Rendel Wyatt, wrote to the Home Office to say they would not continue under the scheme, and returned to [regular] prison, where they stayed until April, 1919.'

By early 1917, camps were being dismantled and men were transferred. Various people outside the NCF began to act and make their thoughts known on the scheme. There was an increasing awareness of who exactly these prisoners were and what they were suffering; a letter written to the *Manchester Guardian* has this, for instance, 'What outlet did the Home Office find for these men, who are drawn from the thoughtful section of the community, whether they be doctors, accountants, university men … or tradesmen and skilled artisans … not only is the work futile, but the conditions under which it is performed are those most calculated to discourage the worker.'

These men were, in most cases, of various religious persuasions, and were very devout and determined in following the precepts of their respective faiths; furthermore, there were diverse minority groups within these numbers. One instance of this will illustrate the predicament of spiritual, morally sound people who stood by their beliefs – the case of the International Bible Students. Their names were listed in the official publications of the NCF, but the first printed material tells the modern reader very little about them. Now, fortunately, researchers have shed more light on those named. Perhaps most typical of these men is Atkinson Padgett from Morley, near Leeds. Born in 1887, he made an attestation in 1915 under the Derby Scheme; but soon after that he read a tract from a student in the IBSA group and gained a radical new credo. Consequently, when the call came for recruitment, he refused. He was court-martialled and imprisoned. To the inspecting tribunal his profile would have seemed to represent the type of applicant who had conveniently acquired religious beliefs when the threat of conscription came along; in fact he was seriously engaged with his religion. He did agree to do some medical support work at the front. But of course, being under martial regulations, it was a serious offence to refuse to carry on, and he was destined to be given the crushing punishment of five years penal servitude at the military prison in Rouen.

Research by IBSA historians, looking at *The Watchtower* for 1916, shows that in July 1916 there were sixty students in prison, another sixty in work centres and twenty non-combatants; by October, 154 were in the Home Office scheme, and there were a total of 254 ISBA men in prison or in camps. Their situation within the standard CO process of tribunals and punishment was that, 'Their services are available to the public weal if permitted to undertake work apart from military control ... This was consistent with their understanding of the Bible, as was their determination not to fight.'

For a human testimony on the settlement experience of the IBSA men, we can refer to the memoir of Jenny Sanderson: 'My husband felt strongly about not taking part in war and by taking such a course he was arrested ... Even though he suffered badly from rheumatoid arthritis he was put in prison, later to spend a year in Dartmoor prison breaking stones ... The villagers were most bitter and hostile to us, even to the point of throwing things at us.'

The settlements were scattered across Britain in a number of barren or isolated places: Denton, Loch Awe, Sunk Island (on the Humber) and Hornsea; but they were also at Chelsea, Grimsby and elsewhere. They were never intended to be anything but temporary. There were many in Wales, where quarrying was the usual occupation. Harvey, the NCF historian, adds to this, 'There was also a road-making gang at Ballachulish, a well-known Highland spot. That included the local schoolmaster, turned navvy.'

Harvey gathered evidence of the kind of menial work done at a number of places, including one where the work was, 'The crushing of oats', which was 'performed with antiquated machinery of the treadmill type arranged for hands instead of feet. Sixteen men are needed to work this machine and the output is six bags a day.' Harvey goes on to provide a full list of deaths, and the most poignant are to be found in the footnotes, such as:

Sentenced to death in France, June 1916. Worked under the Home Office scheme at Dyce; left it on 12 September 1917. Drowned in the River Ouse.

Died at Red Roses camp, Carmarthenshire, of influenza under terrible conditions of crowding and neglect. Peddieson strove to nurse the others in the epidemic, in spite of the Agent's obstructions and insults, till he collapsed himself.

Died of consumption at Wakefield, 17 May 1917, due to the cold at Wormwood Scrubs.

5

THE INTELLECTUALS, RESISTANCE
AND PACIFISM

In 1914, the world of literature and the arts was, in its more wealthy and comfortable echelons, relishing its privileged isolation, secure from the vagaries of the ongoing war. There were parties, dinners, talks, centenaries, and most of all, literary clubs. They were either formal associations, holding their meetings in swanky hotels, or they were coteries who met at the homes of the well-heeled. Patrons rubbed shoulders with university graduates who wanted a literary career; those writers and artists who had won a place in the establishment formed their own societies and circles of friends. Such milieus, perhaps somewhat critically termed the chattering classes, generally had not only a fashionable affection for German culture and literature, but in many cases the British writers had formed friendships with German peers. Hence there were problems when, in the build-up to war, anti-German talk abounded, and the common perception of Germany was that it was a militaristic aggressor.

It comes as no surprise to see that for several writers who became objectors or at least held views sympathetic to objectors, ways were going to have to be found to either participate in anti-war activity or to simply escape – to retreat from the pressing moment.

*

If the resistance to militarism in 1914 was partly an intellectual attitude, then where do the writers, speakers and thinkers belong in this consideration? In some ways, they have had a bad press. One of the most well-known anecdotes is of the writer Lytton Strachey and his experience at a tribunal, testing his application to refuse conscription. When asked by a member of the panel what he would do if a German soldier tried to rape his sister, Lytton replied, 'I would try to position myself between them.'

By the very nature of their professional activity, creative writers, journalists and philosophers have an element of restless dissent in what they produce. Intellectuals will always pose certain problems to those with autocratic power, and in the First World War, it was DORA that enabled the political class to act against any writers whose work might adversely affect national morale, or whose thoughts and writings might be seen as subversive. Yet subverting normal lines of thought is the métier of most novelists and poets, and in the case of 1914–18, that war emerged at a time when British writing was in the thrall of what we now label the modernist period. Writers such as Virginia Woolf, James Joyce, T. S. Eliot and Ezra Pound were challenging the supposedly limited art of their Victorian antecedents in matters of how reality was presented and understood. In other words, they were interested in a fragmented sense of self and in the interior monologue of our consciousness. All this was rather anarchic and unstable at a time when simplicity and stability was something that would assist the undertaking of defeating the Kaiser's hordes.

There were all kinds of minority group thinkers or strong individualists who adopted a stance against the war and were consequently seen as being on the fringes of dissident groups, ploughing their own furrow. Such a dissenter, for example, was Muriel Lester, the daughter of a wealthy industrialist, who developed a close friendship with Nellie Dowell, a poor Londoner who had been brought up in an orphanage. Muriel, always searching for a good cause, inherited money from her father, and then went on to establish a pacifist settlement in Bow, named after Muriel's recently dead brother, Kingsley. In it they ran schools for adults, baby clinics and Montessori classes. But there was nothing solemn or pious about the enterprise. In fact, they included fun nights, with singing and dancing, eschewing all religious or ascetic overtones. Following this early experiment, however, later in life in the 1920s, Muriel began working for the Fellowship of Reconciliation, a pacifist Christian group, creating a second version of her Kingsley Hall as a base.

At the heart of high literary culture in the war period was the Bloomsbury Group; the people who gathered around Ottoline Morrell and Virginia Woolf were open to satire, so much was their evident insularity. Roy Campbell's skit, 'Home Thoughts on Bloomsbury', captures this attitude:

> Of all the clever people round me here
> I most delight in me –
> Mine is the only voice I hear,
> And mine the only face I see.

These kinds of facile judgements were easy to make in a world in which commitment was expected. On the eve of the war,

Edwardian England was not only glutted with writers and aspiring writers all wanting to play their part in the massive expansion of the popular literary presses, it was also a social scene brimming with any number of intellectual and aesthetic pursuits. As Caroline Moorehead puts it, 'Edwardian England was awash with mystical humanists, Theosophists, Christian Scientists, Socialist theologians and preachers preparing for the Second Coming.' Related to this, but more related to actual social action, was the work of intellectuals in the settlements for the poor. The arts graduates were drawn to social action, and the opportunities readily presented themselves. When war came, it was a natural progression for them to be aligned with pacifist thinking, particularly if they were of a socialist frame of mind.

On 18 February 1918, Marie Belloc-Lowndes, sister of the writer Hilaire Belloc, sat with her friends and enjoyed a discussion on politics. She was sitting in The Thirty Club, around the corner from Grosvenor Square in London, as she recorded in her diary: 'I sat between Lady Stanley and Fanny Prothero ... There was a good deal of talk about the effect of war on human beings. Marie de Rothschild told us that she had heard the Germans had a hundred submarines.'

There are many remarkable aspects to note about that chat. First, the club was (and is) exclusively for women, and was originally intended for women in the advertising industry; second, that the women were talking about a traditionally male preserve – the men would talk of submarines after dinner when they had adjourned to a separate room for brandy and cigars – and also that aristocrats and commoners were talking at their leisure. All these points hint at a new world of social relations.

The talk they indulged in was of current topics, issues of the day. The women in Marie's circle were intelligent, freethinking, politically committed; if we ask what had occasioned this intellectual milieu, then the answer lies partly in the notion of service. Beatrice Webb, in her autobiography, suggests that from the late Victorian period there was a transference of the ideals of shared beliefs into a more dominant notion of civic service. In other words, there was a new sense that serving 'man' – working for the personal and social betterment of fellow creatures – was taking over from God-centred Christian morality.

A century earlier, when the Evangelical movement and the crusades of Methodism and Quakerism were at their peak, charity permeated everywhere, seeking to help and serve the labouring 'underclass' spawned by the Industrial Revolution and its great shifts in population and settlement. The millions of publications of the Society for the Promotion of Christian Knowledge established the place of reading and education as central to this charity and reform. Concomitant to this, with science experiencing its own revolution after the famous challenge of Darwin and his peers, mankind itself assumed a new importance within the scheme of things.

Beatrice Webb saw that a new kind of secular, civic service was engendered in this paradigm shift; so, when women began to enter higher education, and the fight for degree qualifications and entry to the professions escalated, there was already a modern habit of being mentally equipped to face the opposition.

A typical example of this new civil attitude in action was that involved in the Women's Industrial Council in the years 1889–1914. In 1889 the Women's Trade Union Association was founded 'to establish self-managed and self-supporting trade unions', and along with such ideals came the everyday tasks associated with helping and advising women at work in industry. The first report of the WTUA covered such trades as tailoresses, mantle makers, shirt makers and umbrella makers. Not only was practical advice given to members, but also a course of lectures was provided; these lecture topics tell us clearly that there existed, as part of the union work, a fair repository of legal knowledge. For instance, the following topics were included in the lectures given to working women: The Labour Laws of Australasia, The Minimum Wage, Separate Courts of Justice For Children, Prison Reform and The Employment of Children Act.

In the range of social and political activities involved in the fight for female suffrage and workers' rights, knowledge of the law was increasingly important, and women were well aware of this fact. This may be seen in the ranks of the Actresses Franchise League; formed in 1908, with the aim of staging propaganda plays and giving lectures, in its ranks were products of the new liberal generation, some of them graduates. Beatrice Harraden, for instance, gained a BA degree with honours in classics and maths at Bedford College, and Violet Hunt, one of the founders of the Women Writers' Suffrage League, was another member. Inevitably, these women would learn a great deal about law and administration. This political education provided a foundation for future openings in the careers comprising the justice system. In fact, Rose Lamartine Yates, a graduate of Royal Holloway College, married a lawyer, Tom Yates, and as Irene Cockcroft has written, 'She studied law with Tom in order to help him with his law practice. In doing so she became aware of the inequity in law between men and women.'

This was a well-established resource for progressive thinking, encouraging a confluence of radicalism, anti-nationalism and pacifism. The NCF could call on a very wide selection of thinkers and writers.

Naturally, these intellectuals would be among the thousands who stood in the tribunals to challenge conscription. Some could, of course, be put to the service of the war effort, used for propaganda; but many saw writers as forces for anarchy and disintegration. The lessons of British history showed that at times of national crisis and emergency the radicals and freethinkers were those who printed seditious material, spoke in public and roused the ignorant to action – in short, those who stirred up the multitude. History also demonstrated that governments had dealt with this problem by locking up the writers and withdrawing their basic human rights, so that trials might not even be expedient in order to put away the troublemakers.

With this in mind, it comes as no surprise that the writers, thinkers and artistic people in all areas were – and are – difficult to fix in the movement of conscientious objection. When researching this element of the subject, certain footnotes of literary history recur. For instance, the influential professor and critic, F. R. Leavis, was a noted non-combatant, serving as a stretcher-bearer, and as one biographer explains, the trench experience was a lasting trauma for him:

He was just nineteen when Britain declared war ... Not wanting to kill, he became a stretcher-bearer with the Friends' Ambulance Unit ... Carrying a copy of Milton's poems in his rucksack ... Meeting trains loaded with wounded soldiers, he had to give as much help and as much reassurance as he could. They were men of his own age. Among them he would find faces that he knew from school and from the town. He has described how 'those innumerable boy subalterns who figured in the Roll of Honour as 'fallen officers' had climbed out and gone forward ... to be mown down.

It is a clear and obvious consequence of sensitive and reflective men facing the barbarity of war, that their conclusions would be critical as well as often lyrical, melancholy and poetic. There is no doubt that Leavis's experience and the influence the war left on his sensibility and reason was something that needed to be voiced. Therein lies the special license of the writers and thinkers who did not fight – they actually expressed feelings, thoughts and opinions. In spite of the strictures of DORA, in the community of writers, editors and publishers there was a literature of feeling, a body of writing busily being circulated about the close-up experience of being asked, cajoled and often bullied into facing a tribunal and, in many cases, working as a non-combatant like Leavis.

Lytton Strachey's life and writings provide an interesting example of the status of writers with regard to the horrendous reality of the war and its mass slaughter. He was in the heart of the Bloomsbury Group, the aforementioned tag which has been attached to the group of writers and socialites whose most celebrated members were Virginia Woolf, Clive Bell, Roger Fry, the philosopher, Bertrand Russell, and the economist, John Maynard Keynes. As Margaret Drabble notes, they 'profoundly affected the development of the avant-garde in art and literature in Britain.'

Strachey makes an excellent example of their refined sensibilities in the face of the brutality of war. His biographer, Michael Holroyd, points out that in the First World War, 'the Bloomsbury Group was advertised as a left-wing pressure organisation which aimed at taking over the Labour Party and establishing an intellectual dictatorship ... It was darkly hinted that they had built up a sinister hold over the press.' He adds that they were seen after 1916 as 'agricultural pacifists and rustic conscientious objectors', and that 'hostility towards them greatly intensified, and ardent-eyed patriots, who had hitherto dismissed the group as a bunch of harmless prigs, now pointed at them with alarm to the explosive danger ... of an obviously pro-German force.'

If we need an example of this, then a look at D. H. Lawrence's experience of going to a medical examination at Bodmin while living in Cornwall will be useful. One writer explains that the potential recruits were 'lined up at the station and marched through the streets to a barracks, and to Lawrence's dismay made to stay overnight. He had not brought any pyjamas ... he had to put up with the teasing of the younger men who saw his beard and called him "Dad".' He told a friend about it and said it was 'a sticky male mess. I should die in a week if they made me a soldier. Thirty men in their shirts, being weighed like sheep, one after the other.' He was given a complete exemption on the grounds of ill health.

What must be noted here, with Strachey in mind as an example, is that in England writers and intellectuals had encountered a persistent attitude of anti-intellectualism, and had been seen as rather irrelevant by a large segment of the population. With the exception of writers such as Dickens, who was clearly socially engaged and wrote immersed in the life of the common people around him, writers in England in 1914 were rather marginal figures. If we compare them to the status of writers in Tsarist Russia, for instance, the contrast becomes clear. The Russian writers such as Tolstoy, Gogol and Chekhov were valued as intellectuals – men whose opinion on social and political matters counted. Chekhov went on an investigative trip to the prison settlement at Sakhalin to document conditions there. He was a medical doctor as well as a writer and playwright, and his reflections were widely valued by his compatriots.

In complete contrast, as literary historians have shown, Britain had a tendency to create in its media a split between the writing community and the readership of literature. A formative piece of research in this respect was John Carey's 1992 study, *The Intellectuals and the Masses*, in which he examines these 'two cultures' in the world of writing and reading. Ian Hamilton, in a review of the book, adumbrates the issue: 'The new literacy had no sooner arrived than it had come under the guidance and control of a new set of tribal chiefs, with Lord Northcliffe and the editor of *Tit-Bits* at its head. There had rapidly come into being what John Carey describes as '"an alternative culture which bypassed the intellectual and made him redundant." It was a culture that used itself up as it went along, but its audience could be numbered in millions and the delights it provided were not all that easy to distinguish from those which the old high culture used to have on offer.' In other words, the new popular literature was everywhere and potent – it carried with it a desire to inform and instruct, yet in doing so it created a certain mass world view – one in which pleasure and adventure were paramount. The influence of this populism hovers over Kitchener's new battalions – known as the Pals Battalions, many called themselves chums after the popular male magazine called simply *Chums*.

As literary culture had developed in Britain through the Victorian and Edwardian years, the kind of writers who believed in the special aesthetic quality of writing and in high literary standards were defined as 'highbrows', a distant and marginalised cadre. They could go to their clubs and dinners, give talks to their groups and so on, but they were hardly seen as a source of much import when it came to the public question of conscription.

Lytton Strachey wrote one of the acutest and most perceptive accounts of this sense of social separation experienced by the Bloomsbury set. In his essay *Monday June 26th 1916* he presents a detailed account of one day in the life of a highbrow writer, with the presence (though rather distant) of the war that consumes youth and destroys love. The essay was written when he was staying on a farm, Wissett Lodge in Suffolk. Strachey had written, expressing the sentiments contained in the essay, in a letter to John Maynard Keynes, 'It is horrid to sit helpless while those poor creatures [soldiers at the front] are going through such things. But really, one would have to be God Almighty to be of any effective use.' Strachey had been given exemption on the grounds of his medical unfitness for conscription.

His essay develops his lyrical statement about writing's need to cleave very close to the experience of life as it is felt by the individual, written honestly and fearlessly. He continues, 'to realize absolutely the events of a single and not extraordinary day – surely that might be no less marvellous than a novel or even a poem', but avers, 'But one can't of course.' Nevertheless, Strachey takes the reader through a sequence of mundane events; he adds two elements which give the piece a highly effective insight into how war infiltrates the imagination at a deep level. The first material relates to a 'vision of that young postman with the fair hair and lovely country complexion who had said "Good evening sir" as he passed on his bicycle,' and the second is a disturbing vision of a boxing match which contains the following powerful description of his response to reading in the *Daily Mirror* about the coming fight:

As for the *Daily Mirror,* what could there be to interest me in that? A face perhaps ... but for weeks past I had never found a single one that wasn't disgusting ... I had found some living creature in it – usually killed. And then I did come on a face – a charming one – of a young boxer – Jimmy Wilde ... I longed to go and see him boxing: I have never seen a boxing match. What would happen? I wondered. Would the blood pour down over his eyes?

On the one hand we have Strachey being drawn to the young post boy, a personal attraction so becoming a search for idyllic beauty; in contrast we have a brutal vision of physical suffering in the harsh masculine world of the war raging over the Channel, distant from his Suffolk home.

The reader feels that, contained within the passages about the post boy and the fight there is an aching, troubled feeling deep inside Strachey that echoes a number of alienations in his life – from maleness, from the 'test' of responding to a war, and also, as he is homosexual, the fundamental apartness (then) from the norm. After all, in most of the cartoons and satires about COs at the time, they were typically depicted as effete, fragile and cowardly, afraid of any 'manly' virtue they were supposed to possess.

That sense of apartness permeates other Bloomsbury writings too. The writers gathered under that name unapologetically saw literature as highbrow, whereas mass study of literature in Britain in the late Victorian and Edwardian eras makes it clear that, for the new mass readership which had been created in the generation after the establishment of national elementary education in 1870, a 'good read' was some form of popular narrative: male adventure and war stories for the boys and romances for the girls. In popular writing the reader expectation is for a straightforward story, a page-turner; in contrast, the Bloomsbury definition of writing was to present the complexity of feeling and perceptions, conscious and unconscious, integrated into an aesthetic unity rather than anything as simplistic as a plot.

In a popular narrative, ideology may be smoothly built into the tale – in both words and pictures. The pursuit of reading in that period generally led to a moral conclusion, to a lesson, or to the reinforcement of ideologies which conformed to conventional notions of moral values and correct behaviour and attitudes.

For all these reasons, writers, thinkers, philosophers and other public intellectuals found their attitudes to the war to be complex. Liberal thinkers, ostensibly immersed in progressive ideals, reverted to the mainstream thought when war arrived. An instance of this is the Church of England Peace League, founded in 1910. It had just a hundred members in its first year of existence, presided over by the Bishop of Lincoln, Edward Hicks. Its aims were 'to keep prominently before the members of the Church of England the duty of combating the war-spirit as contrary to the spirit of Christianity, and of working for peace among nations'. Then as war was declared, as Bishop Hicks noted in his diary, we have this: 'called on the Dean who is eager for war and for fighting Germany [he had been vice president of the Peace League] and he was in a highly warlike mood. He goes on drill and is beating up recruits etc.' Fenner Brockway found a similar trend, noting in his autobiography that lots of journalists who had expressed anti-war sentiments in 1912 were keen for the fight in 1914.

The writers faced with conscription were forced into confronting their true attitudes regarding the war; those who had to face a tribunal had to justify that they could pursue important and productive work. A typical example of this is the case of Duncan Grant and David Garnett, who failed their first application to a tribunal, but then began work as farm labourers at Charleston in Sussex, a place which had been founded by Virginia Woolf and made into a new Bloomsbury Group centre. (Previously a recognised focus for the group had been at the home of Philip and Ottoline Morrell, at Garsington, Oxford.)

The Morrell set mixed regularly with politicians. The prime minister in 1914, H. H. Asquith, as we know from his letters to Venetia Stanley, was a regular visitor on familiar terms at the Morrells. For instance, he wrote just before the outbreak of war, 'Don't, if you can avoid it, go on this infernal river trip, but do come to Ottoline's. Couldn't you even manage dinner there?'

Ottoline's circle had a close association with the people involved in war resistance; there is no doubt that she and her circle provided shelter, advice and useful contacts for the intellectuals who found themselves in difficulties with regard to the tribunals. Bertrand Russell gives a glimpse into what it was like at Garsington when the Morrells were entertaining guests. It was a venerable gathering of the literati:

> At Christmas I went to stay at Garsington, where there was a large party. Keynes was there, and read a marriage service over two dogs … Lytton Strachey was there and read us the manuscript of *Eminent Victorians*. Katherine Mansfield and Middleton Murry were also there. I had just met them before, but it was at this time I got to know her well … Her talk was marvellous, much better than her writing, especially when she was telling of things that she was going to write.

The responses to war and militarism by writers in the popular press had one distinctive feature – it was explicit and direct. In contrast to the ironic subtleties of Strachey's book, in publications such as *Industrial Worker* we have this anonymous poem – a piece in the underground tradition of radical proletarian writers:

I Love My Arms and Legs

I love my flag, I do, I do, which floats upon the breeze.
I also love my arms and legs, and neck and nose and knees.
One little shell might spoil them all or give them such a twist,
They would be no use to me; I guess I won't enlist

I love my country, yes I do; I hope her folks do well.
Without our arms and legs and things, I think we'd look like hell.
Young men with faces half shot off are unfit to be kissed.
I've read in books it spoils their looks; I guess I won't enlist.

If we contrast Strachey's style with this poem, the two pieces reveal the great chasm between the different approaches and responses prompted by war. The war resisters knew exactly what the nature of protest was, and their writings express philosophical reflections for the most part; then there were the poets, and they had at their disposal the strong, rhetorical or satirical forms such as the poem quoted. All the other very consciously literary forms were there, and naturally, with such highly emotional material, a register of lyrical and poetic expression was called for in many cases.

Another interesting dimension for intellectuals and writers is the tendency for the COs in their ranks to suffer professionally. Anyone in this echelon of society who was tenured in academia, or who had a position in such occupations as journalism or arts administration, for instance, was vulnerable. A typical instance of this is in the case of T. H. Parry-Williams, who is today rated very highly in the history of Welsh writing. He was born in 1887, graduating from the University College of Wales, Aberystwyth in 1908. He then acquired a typically academic pan-European training and reading, after studying in Oxford and then at Freiburg, Germany. When the Professor of Welsh died at Aberystwyth, a vacancy for the lectureship became available, and Parry-Williams took it.

When the Military Service Act came in, he registered officially as a CO. At the Appeal Tribunal he was given conditional exemption, as his lectureship was thought to be important work. However, in 1919, at the end of the war, there were two vacant chairs to be appointed at the university for which Parry-Williams was a candidate. Dr Bleddyn Huws, in a magazine feature written in 2015, explains what happened: 'When the college council met in September 1919 to formally appoint the second chair, letters had been received from John Owen, the Bishop of St David's, and from various branches of the Comrades of the Great War, objecting to the appointment.'

There was a manhunt in the newspapers also; one statement in print about Parry-Williams ran, 'I have no love of that "conscience" that refuses to defend the state that protects it, and is eager to snatch the bread out of the mouth of a better man who was first in occupation.'

What followed was a defence by Parry-Williams' father, Henry, who told the world that this treatment was an injustice. A newspaper editor, Morgan Humphreys, agreed to print this defence. Its basic line of argument was that another three of

Henry's sons had been to war, and that his son Thomas Herbert was an outstanding scholar, whose talents should be used to the full in his own university. The result was an impasse. No appointment was made and the matter was deferred for a year. Parry-Williams did a very rare thing: he trained to become a doctor. After a year of medical training, the Welsh chair was again advertised and he was appointed.

This all happened to a man who was described by Dr Bleddyn Huws as 'one of the most prominent poets and writers of the twentieth century Welsh literary renaissance'.

*

If we try to summarise the various responses concerning how the intellectual class saw its predicament in 1914, one of the most incisive statements made was supplied by John Maynard Keynes. It concerns his possible appearance before a tribunal – even though, due to his work at the Treasury being of national importance, he never had to physically attend the proceeding in Holborn. His statement expresses the crux of what we might call 'the thinking person's credo':

> I have a conscientious objection to surrendering my liberty of judgement ... My objection to submit to authority in this matter is truly conscientious. I am not prepared on such an issue as this to surrender my right of decision, as to what is or what is not my duty, to any other person, and I should think it morally wrong to do so.

The important concept here is 'my right of decision'. In the Greek city states of 400 BC, there was no question that every citizen would pick up his sword and spear and join the hoplites to confront the invading Persian hordes. Matters then were simple: fight and survive or perish. That urgency in the heart of war had vanished in 1916. What presented itself instead was a freedom of decision because there was now an established professional army; those citizens who were defined as non-military had a right to decision if asked. It was the coercion on such a matter that felt so profoundly at odds with libertarian notions of the free individual, and further revealed the unequal relationship between the individual and the elected leaders of the state.

As the leaders of the NCF repeatedly insisted, a demand such as civilian conscription was an attack upon 'the soul'. In the end, if we try to understand the position of the writers who came to be war resisters, the bedrock of their condition was a desolate, drifting futility. If they had not openly used their writing skills in support of jingoism and militarism, they were perceived by many as being weak and ineffectual. Lytton Strachey describes this state very strongly in a letter to Francis Birrell in 1915: 'I am alone – desolate and destitute – in a country of overhanging thunderclouds and heavy emptiness. I've got so low that I can hardly bear the thought of anything else, like the prisoners who beg not to be let out of their sentence.' He saw the man in command of the war, and of the nation as a whole, with a critical eye, as most writers did. As Michael Holroyd put it in his biography of Strachey,

> Ultimately, Lytton believed, the world was governed not by extremists, not by flagrantly unreasonable fanatics, but by moderate men. The sight of these men, with their seductive plausibility, in full control of events, posed for him a profoundly menacing spectacle. Their inflated sentiments and headstrong actions presented a terrifying revelation of what the multitudes of ordinary respectable men and women were thinking.

Beneath all the militaristic brainwashing, as many saw it, there was a more basic and primal imperative, known as 'The Test' in the words of Christopher Isherwood, whose father was killed in the war, and who, being born in 1903, was forced to rethink the war at the time of the Armistice and afterwards. In his autobiography, *Lions and Shadows*, he wrote, 'Like most of my generation, I was obsessed by a complex of terrors and longings connected to the idea "war". War, in this purely neurotic sense, meant The Test, the Test of your courage, of your maturity, of your sexual prowess: "Are you really a man?"'

This is important in understanding the thinking of those writers who were opposed to the war, as they stood in a very clear contradistinction to the 'hearty' writers of adventure who saw thrilling storytelling as the real purpose of writing.

There is one outstanding example of conscientious objection in the literary scene of the war, that of Siegfried Sassoon. Here is a case in which a serving officer – and one possessing a Military Cross and Bar – has serious misgivings about the conduct and whole *raison d'être* of the war. In *Memoirs of an Infantry Officer*, we have an account of the gradual intensification of Sassoon's feelings about the sheer waste of life and incompetence in the war. Then, close to the end of that book, when he has decided on 'independent action' as he calls it, he meets a philosopher he calls 'Tyrell' but who is in fact, Bertrand Russell. The scene in which Sassoon contrasts himself with Tyrell is of particular note. Sassoon, it should be recalled, had moved in the literary circles around the Poetry Bookshop, run by J. C. Squire. He had met Rupert Brooke and other Georgian poets, and he was being published. This is the scene in which he begins to formulate the words later used in his famous statement of conscientious objection:

How could I coordinate such diversion of human behaviour, or believe that heroism was its own reward? Something must be put on paper, however, and I re-scrutinised the rough notes I'd been making: Fighting men are victims of a conspiracy among (a) politicians; (b) military caste; (c) people who are making money out of the war. Under this I had scribbled, 'Also personal effort to dissociate myself from intolerant prejudice and conventional complacence of those willing to watch sacrifices of others while they sit safely at home.'

He added after that, 'I am not a conscientious objector. I am a soldier who believes he is acting on behalf of soldiers.' Naturally, he was naive about this – as he was soon to see. As he spoke with Tyrell and composed these notes, he was about to resume service, but not at the front; he was expected to travel to Cambridge and take up the role of instructor to other soldiers. In that new role he would be a responsible link in the chain of what he saw as organised indoctrination.

Sassoon's final statement of objection to the war contained one crucially important statement: 'I am making this statement as an act of wilful defiance of military authority because I believe that the War is being deliberately prolonged by those who have the power to end it.' Infamously, Sassoon threw away his Military Cross. From that moment on, it is through his poetry that we see the expansion and intensification of his thoughts and ideas on the conflict. Still, all this protest was not to end his military career: he was sent to Craiglockhart hospital in Edinburgh where he met fellow war poet, Wilfred Owen, and after that he served again at the front, before being demobbed, as Captain, in March 1919. His poems of protest capture that phase of doubt and criticism very movingly; in some, as in 'Repression of War Experience', he put the case for detesting those in command who sent the youth to war:

> There must be crowds of ghosts among the trees,
> Not people killed in battle – they're in France –
> But horrible shapes in shrouds – old men who died
> Slow, natural deaths, – old men with ugly souls,
> Who wore their bodies out with nasty sins.

The various shades of intellectual participation in conscientious objection provide us with enlightening examples of how the writer and thinker is always, fundamentally, to be looked upon with suspicion in a militaristic state, which is what Britain had effectively become by 1916. This was a nation in which the military's stance of winning the war at all costs could lead to the rough and relentless commandeering of a whole community. One local example will suffice to show what often happened. In his history of Perth in the First World War, Dr Bill Harding offers this summary of the Army's presence in Scotland:

> A measure of army control is seen in the fact that it now controlled no fewer than eighteen hospitals in the Perth area, including Battleby in Redgorton, Aberdalgie and Glenfarg. It was the same with billeting. The military demanded that billeted soldiers have at least 4,300 calories per day, a far healthier diet than that provided by a civilian's 3,859 calories. The calorie intake for troops billeted in Perth was guaranteed by the 'recommended feeding' with five ounces of bread, four ounces of bacon and one pint of tea with milk and sugar for breakfast.

It was a case of civilians sacrificing amenities for the military in all respects. Rules and regulations were ignored and the needs of the community pushed aside. Was it that far from Stalinist Russia, we might ask? A comment by one modern Russian writer is apposite here. Joseph Brodsky wrote, 'A man who sets out to create his own independent world within himself is bound sooner or later to become a foreign body in society and then he becomes subject to all the physical laws of pressure, compression and extremism.' Applied to Britain in 1916, we need only look at those who saw matters of international politics with a longer philosophical view to understand that they were distancing themselves from the supposedly commonsense adage, *if you are not with us, then you are against us*. The enforced groupthink of later totalitarian regimes was not so distant from the First World War mentality in this respect. As W. J. Chamberlain, a member of the NCF committee wrote, 'While DORA was sending men and women to prison for speaking and writing matter "likely to prejudice the discipline of His Majesty's Army", the government were sending hundreds of us into the barracks and camps to preach our gospel with practical illustrations of its effectiveness!'

The fact is that, for the intellectuals in society who saw beyond the immediate patriotic jingoism and the myths and narratives of sacrifice, state repression served only to aid a narrow military chauvinism that operated by bullying, repression and brutality. Brains had no place in soldiering – that was the curt conclusion. Those who obey orders are fine: those who cannot be taught or frightened into obeying orders should be locked up, as they present a threat. Such was the dominant thinking.

6

THE MAJOR FIGURES PROFILED:
FROM BROCKWAY TO RUSSELL

There is no doubt that, in spite of the long list of personnel in the 1919 memorial publication marking the achievements of the NCF, the CO movement was organised and mobilised by certain key figures. There were remarkable people not only at the very top of its structure among the prominent speakers and writers, but also within the regular ranks of the absolutists who suffered long stretches in jail or who stuck out resolutely in the hard labour of the Home Office Scheme. Their biographies provide a rich seam of human experience seldom found in any history of a collective enterprise. But at this stage in my account, there is a call for some of these leading lights to be more fully represented. The following is a series of short profiles of four major figures: Clifford Allen, Fenner Brockway, Bertrand Russell and Alfred Salter. These particular individuals each presented, in their own way, a contribution to the reasoning behind the protest against militarism; each came from different origins, both socially and intellectually. What they shared was a firm belief in there being no argument in favour of, or excuse for, enforced military service.

Fenner Brockway

Fenner Brockway, Honorary Secretary of the NCF, was to become an authority on the British prison system. His study of the prison published in 1922, *English Prisons Today*, co-written with Stephen Hobhouse, is one of the most thorough and readable documents on the subject available, following in the great tradition of Henry Mayhew, who wrote on the prisons of London seventy years earlier. He knew prison life from the inside, thanks to his previous life as a CO during the war.

He was born in Calcutta in 1888 and educated at a missionary school, and, upon moving to London, at an institution which is now known as Eltham College at Mottingham. He became a journalist, writing for a number of periodicals and for the *Daily News*. He joined the ILP in 1907. When the war began, he had firm anti-militarist views.

*

All the absolutists who started a prison sentence did so with a spell in solitary confinement. In Brockway's case, the venue was at HMP Lincoln, on Greetwell Road, well away from the cathedral and the beautiful Roman and medieval core of the upper area of the city. The prison is a typical Victorian local prison – a dispersal jail – and in 1916 it was home to some Sinn Fein men as well as to war resisters like Brockway. The 'block', as it is termed, is tucked away off a lower-level wing, in a corner close to the kitchens. Between solitary cells and the main thoroughfares of Victorian prisons there were other rooms, to allow seclusion as well as close supervision by prison staff. Brockway was faced with the same ordeal as every prisoner had before him – strategies for survival, supports to keep away insanity and dark thoughts. In 1916 there was cold, along with deprivation and little food.

The authorities there were used to problem prisoners. Not long before Brockway arrived, Eamon de Valera and other Sinn Fein men had been kept there after the Easter Rising. (In fact, De Valera, who was there at the same time, was soon to escape, as his support network and local contacts were an efficient bunch.)

Brockway gives an account of his survival strategies in his autobiography:

> Despite confinement to my cell most of the time I felt strangely free. Relaxation came in reading. To last a month I selected the longest books from the library list, wonderfully a volume of Shakespeare's plays, but most of the time I had to be content with instalments of Chambers Encyclopaedia. The Governor allowed me an Esperanto New Testament to replace the Bible and although I had no knowledge of the international language and little of the Gospels, I found I could soon read it easily ... One got tired of reading. Sometimes moments of frustration came, when I wanted to break windows and storm the door.

The Sinn Fein men helped and managed to obtain some journals for him, and also arranged for letters to be sent home to Brockway's wife. Mercifully, he did have one of the most comforting activities a prisoner might hope for – a correspondent who frequently wrote to him. This was Alastar Macaba, the Sinn Fein MP for Sligo.

Brockway wrote, 'Alastar Macaba used to write to me daily. One note indicated that something exciting would happen the following day ... as I got down on my bed board at lights out ... whistles began to blow and doors to bang.' He was hearing De Valera's famous escape.

*

De Valera was a scholarly type, a mathematician. One of his friends at college was Charles Walker, and I have been told of a time much later in De Valera's life when Walker's text books were given to 'Dev' on a day when the famous politician invited Walker's daughter and grandchildren to tea. It says a lot about the man that he was so welcoming, but of course, his life was full of contradictions and puzzles (what politician doesn't have such complexities?). He was born in New York but raised in County Limerick by his grandmother; he was later educated at University College, Dublin, joining the Gaelic League in 1904 and the Irish Volunteers in 1913. He was involved in gun-running at Howth the year after, and commanded the third battalion of the Dublin Brigade in the Easter Rising of 1916.

Before ending up in Lincoln, he had been put in Kilmainham jail after the Easter Rising. There he expected to be shot, writing this note to Mother Gonzaga at Carysfort Convent in Blackrock, where he was a maths teacher: 'I have just been told that I will be shot for my part in the Rebellion. Just a parting line to thank you and all the sisters ... for your unvarying kindness to me in the past ... ' But he was reprieved and lived to see the inside of several other jails in his long political career.

He escaped from Lincoln with two other men, John Milroy and John McGarry. The description given of de Valera at the time says a lot about him, 'aged 35, a professor, standing 6 foot 3 inches and dressed in civilian clothes'. The report emphasised the fact that tracing the men was going to be virtually impossible, 'A close search has been made all over the city, but so far as was known at a late hour last evening the escaped prisoners had not been found.' They were not the only escapees from the Sinn Fein ranks – four men had escaped from Usk prison the week before.

De Valera had been arrested in the 'round up' of May that year, stopped by detectives as he went home to Greystones in County Wicklow. He was then taken across the Irish Sea to Holyhead. The forecast by journalists at the time that he would make his way back to Dublin and 'arrange for a dramatic reappearance in Irish politics' was quite right.

How did they manage to escape? Lincoln prison fronts Greetwell Road, but behind the facility at that time was merely open ground; beyond the rear exercise yards, along the road heading out of Lincoln, there were merely areas for limekilns. The escape was arranged so that full use could be made of the opportunity at the rear. But having said that, there was a constant regime of supervision to contend with, and of course, they needed a master key.

A committee of Irishmen was set up to arrange the escape, who then selected a number of men to do the job. The focus was the aforementioned patch of ground used as the exercise yard. It was surrounded by barbed wire, watched by armed warders in the daylight hours, and patrolled by an Army unit after sunset. Sensibly, the first decision was to decide not to try a direct assault – a rush – as there would have followed an inevitable gun fight. The next plan was to start by finding a way to communicate with De Valera. The solution was to use the Gaelic language.

An Irish prisoner who was working on a garden plot in the jail sang a song, and the words gave De Valera details of the planned breakout. The second time a song was sung it was to direct De Valera to have an impression made of the key that would open the back gate. Today such methods would not be possible, but in the past there was more use made of obligatory outside work, and so there was a degree of vulnerability with regard to the prisoners' enclosure. According to one report, the impression of the key was made with the snatching of a key from a warder to press it into soap, but this seems very unlikely, given the fact that the key would be on a chain and always snapped into a belt-purse when not in use. Far more likely is the theory that a prison chaplain made the impression in soap or in a bread paste. The first two key attempts did not fit, anyway. The third model worked well enough.

The impression was wrapped in brown paper and thrown over the wall; then came the hard part. De Valera would be able to walk through from the main prison building, but there were the sentries to consider. They would have to be distracted, and the way to do that was to use a classic ruse – female allure. Two girls from Ireland were used, as the local girls may well have exposed their plans. *The Lincolnshire Echo* reported that they were 'attractive, vivacious Irish girls, both university graduates, and they were directed to flirt with the guards'. On 3 February, four cars were sent around the country surrounding Lincoln, to create decoys and keep the police occupied; then, at dusk, the Irish girls began to work on the guards. They lured them away from the prison recreation area; the Sinn Feiners then cut through the barbed wire and waited for De Valera to appear: he did, after some initial trouble. The key broke in the lock from the outside, as Michael Collins, who had come to lead the attack, tried to force it, but luckily De Valera managed to force it out from the inside.

They had to move very quickly. Collins and Boland drove straight to the city railway station and caught a train to London. But De Valera and the others split and drove to Manchester.

Like De Valera, Brockway got to know several prisons. He was editing the *Labour Leader* in 1916, and his writing there landed him in court. Fenner and his wife, Lilla, moved to London, but he was living on borrowed time. As he was living with his wife and young child in lodgings he was arrested. His first stretch in Pentonville followed, during which time he was again locked up with another infamous prisoner within the walls – Sir Roger Casement, who was executed for treason while Brockway was there.

Then Brockway went through the hoops of the tribunals. He refused to obey any military order and the result was a visit to yet another jail – this time, Chester Castle. He faced military courts, was sent to Wandsworth, and then returned to Chester. Brockway even spent a night in the Tower of London, a destination at the time reserved for spies who were to be shot for treason. He was by 1917 something of an 'old lag' among the COs and he wrote, on entering prison in Liverpool, 'I entered a new mood. When first imprisoned I was prepared to accept the punishment, proud to undergo it as a witness to anti-war convictions. Now I had no longer the spiritual exaltation of a novice and was not in the temper to accept penalties gladly. I found myself in a hall with sixty other objectors and we developed elaborate plans to overcome the rule which forbade speech and communication.'

Brockway certainly never wasted any time in prison, and although he may have been bored trying to read for long hours, he also wrote. In his remarkable, many-sided life and career, he wrote creatively as well as critically, producing a science fiction novel and drama. While in prison he wrote a play called *The Recruit*, in which he used the freedom of purely imaginative writing to put in print a veiled defence of his political reasoning. When one character, Gould, asks Williams (the Brockway figure in the play) if he is a CO, Williams admits that he is; Gould then puts the question which was being asked at hundreds of tribunals across the land: 'But surely we must defend our nation when it is attacked?' The ensuing answer is arguably one of the clearest and strongest statements on the theme of conscientious objection:

WILLIAMS: I believe that if a nation were sufficiently strong absolutely to put aside all armed defence, it would be secure from all attack. I don't believe there is a people in the world who would march with fire and sword upon another if met with food and flowers instead of shot and shell.

GOULD: Oh come, that is pure speculation. You must act in the world as it is. Given present conditions, how can you stand aside when your country is attacked?

WILLIAMS: You see, I don't believe it is a simple matter of one's country being attacked. Of course, one nation is often more to blame than another, but it does not seem to me that any nation is sufficiently innocent to assume that all the right is on its side.

It would have been very difficult to persuade a Belgian citizen in 1914 that proffering food and flowers would have pushed aside the German army, but then, that is a central issue in pacifist thinking – that only if all relinquished arms, there would be no need to have any wars. But in choosing a play to air his opinions, and dramatising the debates he had had so often in his life, Brockway showed the urgency and expediency of expressing ideas in creative forms.

The ILP opposed the war, and Brockway in his function as editor of the *Labour Leader* gathered contributions from ILP people, such as the very influential Lowes Dickinson (who reappears in my account of Clifford Allen) and Edward Garnett. Brockway as editor and activist was often asked to speak in public; he had at times been viciously attacked on such occasions, but in Glasgow he learned a broader view: 'My visit revealed that opposition to the war in Scotland was based not on "Thou shalt not kill" but on working-class wrongs and international working-class solidarity. The leaders – Maclean, Maxton, Shinwell and Kirkwood – deliberately courted imprisonment and deportation.' He quotes Maxton's song in his autobiography, and it is clear that he admires the forthright and explicit words, such as,

> O I'm Henry Dubb
> And I won't go to war
> Because I don't know
> What they're all fighting for.

The campaign against the ILP went on, just as it was later waged against the NCF; bookshops deemed to be seditious in Manchester and London were raided. The *Labour Leader* was generally tolerated, but it was censored on one occasion, there being a police visit at one time just before an issue was printed, with Fenner and Lilla accompanying officers to Salford police station. Brockway admitted in his autobiography that he wanted the law to delete some text, so that there would be evidence of state censorship. The red pen was applied strongly – a feature by Clive Bell was cut out and an advert was ordered to be erased.

Brockway always took a more international perspective on pacifism, and in his account of his time during the war he refers to communications from such left-wing luminaries in Europe as Karl Liebknecht and Rosa Luxemburg, both fated to be killed in the post-war social disorder. Brockway wrote, 'When I visited Berlin after the war I stood in silent homage before the Eden Hotel where Karl and Rosa were murdered.'

Of all the memoirists from the COs who wrote about the war afterwards, Brockway is the one who takes time to weigh and consider the major figures on the Left at the time. He has plenty to say about Keir Hardie and Ramsay MacDonald. Of Hardie he has no doubt of a major influence then as well as later, praising him in no uncertain terms; 'Devotion to Hardie fired me ... I admired Hardie more deeply than any man I have known in my life. Bernard Shaw gave it direction, Keir Hardie gave it implementation.'

There is no doubt that the prison experience was formative in many ways for Brockway, and at the time of his first arrest he was immersed in the formation and organisation of the NCF. He writes that it succeeded because it knew that a strategy had to be devised to function and survive in spite of the repression. He explains that,

The NCF became an extraordinarily efficient underground movement. We prepared a code so that when we telegraphed that a meeting would be held at Manchester it would be at Newcastle. When the National Labour Press, owned by the ILP, was dismantled by the police for running off our journal, the *Tribunal*, we bought a small press and housed it every week at a different address.

They were well aware of the new intelligence initiatives regarding interception of mail, censorship and actions against spy networks. At the beginning of the war, Vernon Kell, then in charge of MI5, and his team expanded this counter-espionage operation, allowing a spy network to build up before swooping to arrest all participants. The same scenario would happen with the nationwide network of the NCF.

Brockway paid homage, on several occasions, to the other major figures working against conscription. Of Clifford Allen he wrote, 'One's first memory of him was of a simple modesty, soon accompanied by twinkle-eyed humour, becoming an irrepressible Puck.'

Undoubtedly, it was prison that most impacted on Brockway regarding the eventual direction of his future life. His first description of Pentonville – his first incarceration – includes an explanation of exactly what prison work does for a bright individual who must direct all available energy to where it will help survival: 'Our cells at Pentonville were thirteen feet by eight feet, and each contained a bed board, a basin for washing, a pot for sanitary purposes, a shelf for toilet articles, a slate and a Bible. After that we worked for an hour ... and then in our cells sewing mailbags. The daily task was seventy-two feet. At first I could not do ten feet, but before I had finished with prison I could do seventy-two feet in three hours.'

If the modern reader wants to know how the authorities acted on the intellectuals they found in their cells, and how and why the prison staff adapted their approach and application of justice, Brockway gives some insight. Naturally, when it came to handling the dissenting leaders, the Army and the top brass were not simply going to leave them to rot. Brockway details:

An incident then occurred which suggested that the War Office was making a last minute effort to tempt me to compromise. One night I was marched to the Officers' Quarters, welcomed and offered a drink. A senior officer, after casual conversation, assured me that no-one was happy about my imprisonment, and that the authorities wished to avoid it. 'You are an experienced journalist. Why shouldn't you do press work for a department in Whitehall?' I laughed. 'You want me to use my pen for the war when I won't use a gun?' I think the officer saw my point.

As it turned out, he did use his journalistic skills inside – to produce a prison paper for the COs. In Liverpool he managed to produce the *Walton Leader*. Its content was remarkable in many ways, but perhaps most astoundingly in reference to the theatre of war. He explained, 'An incoming Objector brought us a detailed account of the slaughter at Passchendaele written by a deserter who was in the guard room at the same time ... It was ironical that whilst the press outside was not allowed to publish the story, a prison paper was able to do so.'

When released from prison, Brockway became chairman of the No More War Movement, and in that capacity he was glad to be involved with an internationalist cadre, becoming a speaker at a number of events and assemblies. He also had benefactors who asked how they might help. He wrote, 'I replied a house for my family ... he took my breath away by saying he would give me £1,000 to buy one. Thus Lilla and I came to live in Keir Cottage at Thorpe Bay.' While here, in Essex, he was to work with Stephen Hobhouse, who had been very ill and needed help and rest. The two of them worked on *English Prisons Today*; Brockway had previously averred that he had not finished with his prison experience – not until he had put on paper something substantial about the whole establishment.

As for Brockway's own summing-up of the work of the NCF, he knew that future success lay in providing some kind of permanent textual record of the experience of their members. He wrote in 1919, 'It is scarcely possible to exaggerate the value which these records proved to be in the later stages of the struggle.' He was proud, as he reflected on the course of the NCF's progress over the previous five years, that such a high degree of cooperation had been achieved. A disparate group of people had come together and used both tenacity and intellect to survive.

Clifford Allen

Pictures of Clifford Allen show a frail man, and indeed he was physically weak. But in his face it is possible also to read his underlying character – self-assurance, resolution and charm. These are excellent attributes for one whose business is to communicate and create bonds of affiliation, and that is what he could do, as he moved in life from one role to another. In this way, it is as the chairman of the NCF that he will be remembered. His portrait is the first thing to meet the reader's eye on the 1919 memorial booklet for the Fellowship: penetrating eyes and strong chin, a longish face and a rich head of hair; then that severe collar and tie, and an expression of confidence. This was the man who was to impress virtually everyone he met – friends, colleagues, and even those in opposition.

Allen was born in Newport, Monmouthshire, on 9 May 1889. His father ran a drapery firm, and his mother, in the words of

Arthur Marwick, Allen's biographer, was 'a consumptive whose great beauty was set ablaze by the fevered intensity which often goes with that condition'. The Allens were not in South Wales for long, moving to Bournemouth when the boy was only eight. Two years later he was sent to boarding school, at Berkhamstead, where he became Senior Scholar.

He was intended for the church, passing his Bachelor of Divinity exams in Latin (awarded by London University) despite being seriously ill. The frailness that was to dog his life was at that point already evident. But he progressed to university study, first at Bristol, where he was taught by George Hare Leonard, who had a radical turn of mind. There, he and Allen undertook a survey of the poorer parts of the city, in the manner of Charles Booth's monumental study, *Life and Labour of the People of London*.

Leonard was a real influence on Allen's approach to life. He referred to the Professor of Modern History as a 'spiritual godfather'. In 1905 he had read a paper to the Livingstone Society at Oxford which the reviewer of *The Spectator* described as giving 'an eloquent and touching appeal for help in social work'. It was published as *Nobler Cares* in 1909, its central thesis arguing that men are 'called' to the service of God and the State. The reviewer was impressed, concluding that, 'No-one but will be better for reading this book.' Allen, inspired by this, began some work with a settlement, run by the University Settlement Movement. Beatrice Webb, who did similar work, ruminated in her autobiography on the tendency of society generally in her time to reflect the notion that 'the idea of service had been transferred from God to man'. In this, the settlements were a fertile ground for young graduates to make a social contribution and see the more deprived elements in life at close quarters.

Allen learned from this and made his contribution, being restless and eager to be involved wherever he could; he was active in several college societies, for instance. Arthur Marwick points out that he had 'a charm of manner' early in his career, and adds further, 'A fellow student described him as always very tidy and fresh looking in a grey suit, and added that he could always be depended on to participate in social functions.' He was a joiner and a speaker, as well as being an excellent student. He won an Exhibition to Peterhouse College, Cambridge. When he started work there, in 1908, it all but seemed that he was closing in on that clerical career. But Arthur Marwick, in his expertise as a historian of political movements, points out that Allen had meanwhile been deeply influenced – as many were – by the emergence of the Liberals on the one hand and the new Labour Party on the other, in the election of 1906.

The ILP was active and impressed many at that time, including Allen. Cambridge coincidentally had a vibrant Fabian Society, which was, along with the ILP, linked to the Labour Party – then possessing thirty seats in parliament. It was a political movement on the rise, and Allen wanted to ride with the others who were winning. He became an eloquent writer and speaker, as well as working at his networking and alliances. In the Fabian ranks there was the doomed poet, Rupert Brooke, with whom he became friends. Then along came the other person who was to define Allen, with Leonard, as a 'spiritual godfather' – Lowes Dickinson. Here was a man who influenced so many of the people he met. Marwick points out that Dickinson was famously recorded as saying that 'all the creeds are guesses, and bad ones'.

Dickinson ran a publication called *The Independent Review*. This was at a time – the golden age of bookmen and literary journalists in the decade before the war – when there were opportunities for aspiring writers of all shades of opinion. Allen was beginning to see openings and opportunities, in both writing and in politics. His clerical aims withered away, to the dismay of his parents, and he instead became deeply engaged in political debate. Allen spoke in the union at university, and was noticed. In 1910 he spoke on the topic of single-chamber government and won favourable comments from those with status and influence. Then in 1911 he spoke in a debate on collectivist socialism, with the result of 138 votes in favour – something that prompted a comment that the young man's speech had been remarkable.

In 1911, as Allen's father bought a home in London, Allen took his chance and asked to share the place, being an ideal location close to the contacts he had made. He applied for a secretarial post with a new Labour newspaper, and he was appointed. But he did much more. Marwick notes that in April 1912, Allen took it upon himself to arrange a mass meeting of university representatives intended to stir Fabians into more meaningful action. He was thus elected president of a University Socialist Federation. He had arrived, as they say.

The Labour paper, *The Daily Citizen*, took off, and was rival to George Lansbury's paper, *The Daily Herald*. Consequently, by the eve of the war in 1914, Allen was a known figure on the Left. He was prominent in a cluster of important organisations, and he had used his charm and communication skills to become a presence in the ranks of the incipient Labour party. He was secretary to Ramsey MacDonald; he moved in the social circles around the Leftist press and journalism.

When war came, he was the ideal candidate for the leadership of the NCF. He, with Fenner and Lilla Brockway, took the lead in assembling support for anti-war initiatives, Allen thinking that the ILP would take the lead. But he and his friends saw that they themselves would have to make decisive action. In early 1915 the NCF was vibrant, well followed and in need of a broad base. Accordingly, they opened their office in Fleet Street. In a matter of months, things moved swiftly, and at the first full conference in November 1915, Allen made the long speech that was to have a profound influence on the war resistance. His clear explanation of the absolutist stance won great respect:

> The members of the No-Conscription Fellowship base their fundamental objection to conscription on this ground; that whatever else a state may or may not do, whatever infringement of individual liberty a state may or may not effect, there is one interference with individual judgement that no state in the world has any sanction to enforce – that is, to tamper with the unfettered free right of every man to decide for himself the issue of life and death.

He stood before the tribunal in Battersea on 14 March 1916, as was reported in the NCF paper, *Tribunal*. When Allen gave the same response to the standard question about standing by while under attack, the same answer as Brockway had given in his play, *The Recruit,* he was challenged by a tribunal member – the interchange provoked the attending military man to interfere:

> MEMBER OF TRIBUNAL: But assume that Germany should attempt an invasion of this country, what would you suggest should be done?
> ALLEN: I repeat, I could take no part in that war, and if others

shared this view there would be no invasion. Countries invade each other because they are afraid of each other.

CAPT. BRIGGS: Mr Chairman, we have had enough of this. This case should be stopped.

THE CHAIRMAN: I will protect the applicant.

At the end of the tribunal, the clerk said, 'He conducted his case very nicely and very well. It was a pleasure to listen to him.'

As with all the absolutists, prison was his destination. In Allen's case, his weak constitution made him vulnerable to severe illness, so extreme that people feared for his life. He was in that circuitous process of non-stop release and re-arrest that all objectors knew. Consequently, as his prison terms went on, he became progressively sicker. He was a thorn in the side of the prison regimes, being placed in solitary confinement several times, existing on a bread-and-water diet.

Allen contracted tuberculosis and he was at times close to death. Finally, at the end of 1917, he was released. He had served sixteen months behind the prison walls.

Bertrand Russell

Bertrand Russell, polymath and public intellectual, was to become one of the truly great and influential figures of twentieth-century history, with interests, writings, speeches and active involvement in a wide range of activities. His central concerns in the field of philosophy will always be the defining element in his rich and varied life, but in the interests of this present work, he plays a major political role also in the NCF. In the second volume of his extensive autobiography, in which he deals with the years 1914–44, he gives an account of his anti-war work.

By 1919 he was a fellow of the Royal Society, although, conversely, he had been sacked from his university lectureship because of his conscientious objection to the war. In fact, as his profile in the NCF memorial booklet states, 'He was forbidden from lecturing in various parts of the country, and passports to America were refused him, despite the fact that the object of his journey was the fulfilment of an engagement to deliver lectures at Harvard University.' He always had opinions to express, and when the war ended and he was asked for a comment at the last NCF convention, he said that 'during the war two events had given him cause for hope – the Russian Revolution and the stand of the NCF'.

Russell was born in 1872, already a father figure in some ways when it came to wartime discussion and opinion. He was educated at Trinity College, Cambridge, where he became a fellow. Over a decade before war broke out, he had made his name in the higher study of maths with *The Principles of Mathematics* in 1903. This was followed by *Principia Mathematica* in 1910.

In the months just before August 1914, he was in the midst of several social circles which were very much engaged with social and political issues and debate – associations including the earlier mentioned Bloomsbury Group, John Maynard Keynes and several prominent academics. He wrote in his autobiography that the war was to impact on him in many ways, but paradoxically, 'It may seem curious that the war should rejuvenate anybody, but it in fact shook me out of my prejudices and made me think afresh on a number of fundamental questions.' He admitted that he was then 'living in the highest possible' state of 'emotional tension'.

Becoming a militant and standing against the war fever was

not an immediate act for him; he admits that he was 'tortured by patriotism'. He looked around him, following Sir Edward Grey's announcement that there was to be war with Germany, and he saw friends in states of mind that astounded him: 'My best friends, such as the Whiteheads, were savagely warlike.' Then he explains his entrance into the ranks of the NCF. He saw at once that there was a gargantuan task ahead to promote arguments in favour of anti-conscription:

> There was a great deal of work to do, partly in looking after the interests of individuals, partly in keeping a watch upon the military authorities to see that they did not send conscientious objectors to France ... Then there was a great deal of speaking to be done up and down the country. I spent three weeks in the mining areas of Wales ... I never had an interrupted meeting ... In London, however, matters were different.

He was eventually – inevitably – sent for a spell in prison in May 1918. Russell explains the reason, which came after he was asked to write for *Tribunal* magazine, 'I warned that American soldiers would be employed as strike-breakers in England, an occupation to which they were accustomed when in their own country ... I was sentenced for this to six months' imprisonment.'

He was jailed and sent to Brixton. Perhaps his most noted action during that spell inside was his celebrated letter to the *Manchester Guardian* in which he replied to a piece by a certain 'Artifex' who had written, 'I think that to be a real conscientious objector a man must be consciously or unconsciously an extreme individualist with little sense of the solidarity of mankind and of our membership, one of another.' His main statement in response was a brilliant encapsulation of the CO thinking: 'It seems to me that when he wrote "mankind" he was thinking only of the Allies. But the Germans, too, are included among "mankind". The CO does not believe that violence can cure violence, or that militarism can exorcise the spirit of militarism.' He concluded with the rhetorical question, 'Is there really such a vast gulf between Wormwood Scrubs and Ruhleben [the German prison for Allied POWs]?'

There are many outstanding features of Russell's more accessible, popular writing, but two must be selected as being highly useful and relevant to his theme of war resistance: the ability to speak to Joe Public as well as to peers and academics, and the rare ability he had of mixing a detached, documentary angle on his experience with a constant desire to teach and reveal. He was, in this aspect of his many-sided work, fuelled by a didactic aim, but always with an eye on the tendency of facts alone to bore the reader. He appears to have followed Samuel Johnson's axiom that men more often need to be reminded than informed, and tended to express experience to anybody at all. His letters from prison are a case in point: many, written to his brother, form a record of, in essential terms, a typical acclimatisation to life as a prisoner. 'Life here is just like life on an ocean liner; one is cooped up with a number of average human beings, unable to escape except into one's own state-room.' The letters illustrate perfectly what tends to happen when prison is applied as a punishment to those who need intellectual sustenance and personal space – they may even find unexpected benefits. Writers in prison have a certain rare utility. They are literate and articulate, and less well-educated lags have a need to write letters home, send birthday wishes and so on. The

COs were therefore often highly valued by the prison populace. Russell puts it simply: 'Here I have not a care in the world: the rest to will and nerves is heavenly.'

It seems that, as long as the manual, repetitive and pointless labour could be endured, then prison could be a space in life for spiritual renewal, philosophical reflection and a rethinking of opinions and values. All this applies to Russell in Brixton. More than anything else, it gave Russell a chance to read at leisure. One letter gives a survey of his taste, 'Tell Lady Ottoline I have been reading the two books on the Amazon: Tomlinson I loved; Bates bores me while I am reading him, but leaves pictures in my mind which I am glad of afterwards. Tomlinson owes much to *Heart of Darkness*.'

Of course, there was pain and deprivation as well, and while in jail he had a personal problem – his girlfriend Colette had fallen in love with someone else. As prisoners will tell visitors, that horrendous inability to act in such situations is torture. Russell wrote, 'While I was in prison I was tormented by jealousy the whole time.' His relationship with Colette was not actually ended at that time, but he explains, 'We remained lovers until 1920, but we never recaptured the perfection of that last year.'

Russell was well aware of his need to write differently. The academic in him was still there, but he became a great populariser, a provoker of thought – in fact, one might say he acted the role of a Socrates, unsettling any lazy thinking, and more than anything else, writing in such a way that the reader reasons with him towards conclusions, tackling woolly – or illogical – thought along the way. He wrote in his autobiography that he ceased to be academic, and 'took to writing a new kind of book.' He was, as he realised, in a situation which defined him as being in opposition – a mind at odds with the mainstream attitudes. This, as he candidly admits, lost him some friends, but he made new ones. He was sloughing off a skin, so to speak. What emerged was a man who was, in effect, realigning his sense of self and his patterns of thought. He wrote that, by the end of the war, all he had done 'had been totally useless except to myself'. Of course, this is a wild understatement. He achieved a great deal.

Russell was always rather self-critical, but equally he voiced so much that his honesty about himself, his soul-searching, always appeared to be direct and sincere. Regarding his work for the NCF he wrote, in one of his many letters, 'I ought to have gone into more hostile districts. Here [South Wales] it is merely a picnic and I feel I should be better employed in town.' He found the touring to speak again and again to be a hard task, frankly admitting, 'Speaking is a great nervous strain. I feel very slack all the rest of the time. But I sleep well and my mind is at peace.'

By 1919, after he had been to prison, tackled his values and expressed opinions wherever he could, Russell was a more complete, eclectic thinker and writer. What had he contributed to the battle undertaken by the NCF? For one, he had been something of a celebrity figurehead; he had added gravitas and credibility to the cause; he had been able to speak and write in every conceivable context; and he worked extremely well with Allen and Brockway. Being a respected academic and thinker, the fact that his Cambridge lectureship had been taken away could only, in many right-minded circles, be seen as a very negative criticism of the university's leanings. Overall, he was certain that, in identifying himself with the war resisters, it had to be done completely and without any pause for thought. That approach showed through in everything he did.

Alfred Salter

Dr Alfred Salter's statue now stands by the Bermondsey Wall East, produced by Diane Gorvin. The figure stands there, proud and strong, as Alfred was in life. He stood out in NCF group photographs, having a sturdy frame, a rather pugnacious face, with a hat and cane. His whole demeanour suggests determination and security.

He was born in Greenwich in 1875 and became a medical student at Guy's Hospital; but as he was learning medicine he was also absorbing socialist ideas, reading Karl Marx and others. He joined the Social Democratic Federation, along with the Band of Hope, in the 1880s, with temperance being one of the keystones of his thought. He met Ada, who became his wife, while working at the Bermondsey Settlement.

Working as a local doctor, he charged only sixpence for consultations, and became increasingly concerned for local issues, knowing the results of poverty and deprivation at first hand. Like many of his peers, he saw politics in a broad, international perspective. As Fenner Brockway wrote of him, 'His hopes were high when he read of the great working-class demonstrations held in every capital of Europe on the Sunday before war was declared.' He thought that the German Social Democrats would prevail in any talk of war, but he was wrong.

When that apparent European solidarity crumbled, it was a deep shock to him. The fact is that he was a Christian deep in his bones: his political beliefs were founded in the religion, and so pacifist thinking naturally ran through him, and imbued everything he said and wrote with Christian feeling and morality. When it came to the declaration of war with Germany, he felt that the best way to express his pacifism was through a line of thought grounded in the notion of faith; and his essay, 'Faith of a Pacifist', was a seminal statement for the NCF. Brockway tells the story of its genesis:

> He sent it to the Labour Leader for publication; the author of this book was then editor of the ILP organ and he still remembers the effect of reading Salter's words – the startling courage and the shattering strength of them; never had he read anything more challenging or powerful … The forthrightness of this article would invite prosecution – but would it? Would any government dare to draw the attention of the whole nation to this convincing assertion that no Christian could take part in war?

Salter wrote of 'the Son of God with a machine-gun' and 'The Man of Sorrows in a cavalry charge', and of course, such thinking made him susceptible to a charge of being pro-German. He was accused by many and defended by many, as his humane doctoring and his evident sense of actually caring about the poor won him many friends. The anti-German feeling was so strong, exacerbated by the sinking of the *Lusitania,* as has been discussed earlier, that perhaps Salter, with his friend, the Revd Kaye Dunn, should have refrained from speaking in public at the time of such xenophobia. But they did – at a meeting in Beatrice Road. Dunn was already known as someone who had holidayed in Germany before the war, and had written about that country glowingly in his parish magazine. Now here were two pro-Germans, many locals thought, addressing them publicly about the wrongness of the war. There was trouble, of course. There were shouts of 'hang him to a lamp-post', and Brockway comments, in his life of Salter, 'Had not Dr Salter been at his side, he [Dunn] would have been assaulted. This was only the beginning of the campaign of violence against the minister.'

Salter was never scared of the mass thought against him. After one such confrontation, involving more of his friends, Salter experienced violence at first-hand, on his very doorstep. Brockway describes what happened:

An angry crowd gathered in front of his home in Storks Road and began to throw bricks. Salter flung open the door and faced the mob from his steps. He silenced them by the audacity of his action and his righteous anger ... 'They slunk away,' reports one witness of the incident, 'as though the doctor had lashed them with whips rather than words.'

His exposure and involvement with the NCF started when the ILP gave its support to COs in Bermondsey, and Salter joined up as an associate member; a local branch of the ILP was then created. That branch then commenced a fund to support COs in prison, with Ada and Alfred at the heart of the campaign.

As Salter became more engaged with the issues confronted by the NCF, there was an early crisis. Brockway explains what this was:

The NCF had to face an organisational problem which no society had confronted before. Since its entire membership was composed of men pledged to resist a contemplated Act of Parliament, there was the prospect that at some point the organisation would disappear because its personnel would be behind bars! ... members and officers of the Fellowship were scattered to remote places, and the original organisation was dispersed beyond recognition.

The readjustments and efforts to remedy this entailed hard work by the leaders, among whose number was Salter, and he worked with several individual cases who were savagely handled by the tribunals. Brockway sums up, 'Dr Salter was a tower of strength ... he appeared to enjoy the conflict with the military and with the authorities; he was never overcome by any situation, and his irrepressible cheerfulness and Homeric laughter kept all his colleagues in good spirits.'

If one had to isolate a contribution that Salter made to the NCF work which stands out, it would be his pastoral and therapeutic work, he and Ada being deeply involved in the restitution of Bermondsey's people, back into a life of security and health from the low condition many were in through economic circumstances. He had his chance when he acquired Fairby Grange, a country house which he had found in a ruinous state while he was on a country walk. This was to become his own personal convalescent home and general retreat for those in need. Brockway summarises this neatly, 'He decided to make Fairby Grange into a convalescent home for his Bermondsey patients without fees.' He also gives some examples of typical clients, 'There came poor women from Bermondsey, pale and thin from the endless labour of caring for a large family in a small slum tenement; there came consumptives for whom sleeping places were built in the grounds; a little girl came who looked about the green countryside bewildered and asked where were the gates.'

Salter summed up the 'religion' of a CO as being a spiritual one in the face of the 'materialist' one of 'big battalions, millions of armed men, the superiority of artillery, the efficiency of organisation'. The other religion, he insists, is that which teaches that 'the cause of right wins in the long run'.

There is no denying that Alfred Salter singularly pursued this vision, and feared nothing. It is tempting to conclude this profile of him by saying that he was a muscular Christian turned to stopping war rather than simply running a crusade for healthy sport and hymns several times a day. That would perhaps be too extreme; he was, in the end, a man who advocated reason and moderation.

These leaders each had their own virtues and strengths, and it is easy to see how a successful team was built in 1914. Now would be an opportune moment to detail the story of the reserve squad on the bench, as it were, the women members – as fully informed and equally as determined as their male counterparts in the fight to resist conscription.

7

THE WOMEN AND THE CAUSE

Almost a year before the first Military Service Act came into force, the presence of women in the movement for peace had been observed in a large-scale event – a conference at The Hague in April 1915, which lasted for three days and comprised women delegates from twelve countries. It had been established by Dutch women, who freely stated that the assembly would go ahead regardless of who could come to join in. At that juncture travelling to The Hague was no easy task. War was waging all around. From Britain, 180 women wanted to go, but only twenty-five were given passports. Even then, crossing the Channel was not possible for most of their number, due to problems with crossing arrangements. There was an interruption of passenger traffic, for one – only to be expected in wartime. In the end, four British women attended for the International Women's Congress, the three known ones being Chrystal Macmillan, Emmeline Pethick-Lawrence and Kathleen Courtney. International cooperation was one of the agreed aims, and of course, communication between groups, effected in any way possible.

The Times reported that, 'It is not the intention of those promoting it to call for peace at the moment or to end the war – a task obviously beyond their power ... On the contrary, discussion on the national responsibility for, or conduct of, the present war will be ruled out of order.'

The women of the British Committee told the press that they were pressing for an amendment to the various resolutions, including one calling for the definition of peace terms which would make it read as follows:

> Since the people in each of the countries now at war believe themselves to be fighting not as aggressors but in self-defence and for their national existence, this International Congress of Women urges the governments of the belligerent countries to (a) publicly define the terms on which they are willing to make peace, and (b) to open negotiations at the earliest possible moment and to refuse any proposal not to do so.

The woman at the heart of all this for Britain was Chrystal Macmillan, one of the first female barristers and a Scottish Liberal, born in 1872. At the beginning of the war, she became prominent in the International Women's movement, and after the 1915 event, she was elected to visit several countries on behalf of the organisation; she spoke with state leaders, and eventually, when President Woodrow Wilson created his Fourteen Points – a precursor to the creation of the League of Nations – the Hague resolutions figured in the thinking. Macmillan, at the end of the war in 1919, appeared again at another major peace conference in Paris.

In Macmillan, the International group had an exceptionally talented woman. She had degree-level qualifications in Mathematics as well as in Law, and she also studied in Germany in the 1890s. She was deeply involved in the movement for women's rights before the war, and was in the same group as some of the prominent NCF members – the National Union of Women's Suffrage Societies. When it came to being militant for peace, she was not idle: in 1914 she travelled on a mercy mission to Holland, and then worked hard to help war refugees in Antwerp. She soon became active in movements for international communication and cooperation.

The 1915 assembly certainly made general readers of the papers aware that women were working for peace, in contradistinction to traditional perceptions of women being nurses or support workers, backing up militarism in the eyes of the NCF.

*

The first glimpse the general reader tends to have of women involved in the CO organisations is largely in retrospective publications. There is no doubt that a central core of women writers and campaigners played a pivotal role in the movement, notably in the work of the NCF.

Arguably the most prominent is Catherine Marshall. Fortunately, Jo Vellacott Newberry has written and researched extensively on Catherine Marshall since the mid-1970s, and thanks to her efforts, her name is now more widely known and her contribution to the NCF better appreciated. In the memorial publication of the NCF she figured along with several other women campaigners; Marshall was recognised as a notably vibrant and committed member of the Fellowship:

To our first Convention Catherine E. Marshall came as the Fraternal Delegate of the Women's International League, and she was so impressed by the spirit there revealed that she decided to devote the whole of her services to our movement. She became Parliamentary Secretary and later Acting Hon. Secretary of the Fellowship. It was her determined will that built up the Parliamentary Department of the NCF, so that our stand was never without a champion in the House of Commons or the House of Lords.

Jo Vellacott, in a lecture given in 2014 at Somerville College, explained that her interest in Marshall began when she followed up an initial curiosity by looking at the Marshall archive in Carlisle which consisted of some forty boxes of material. Her comments on that experience give a first impression of Marshall's character: 'They were unsorted and there were no funds available to resolve that, and so I sorted them myself, which took forever! My focus then was the anti-conscription movement but I would later return to the archive as it had lots of material on the women's suffrage movement too.' She concluded, 'It matters to keep the story of Catherine Marshall alive ... Marshall would have liked a strong educational programme to look at better ways of making internal decisions ... She wanted to pursue peacemaking on the basis not of hatred and vindictiveness but on something that would last.'

Catherine Marshall was the one who, as W. J. Chamberlain recalled, filled the vacancy of administration work at the crucially important moment: 'A shadow committee was chosen ... this precaution was taken in the case of everybody who had any work to do in connection with the Fellowship, so that no matter who was taken, the work was carried on ... the women stepped into the breach, led by Miss Catherine Marshall.'

Marshall was born in 1880 and was educated at the prestigious boarding school of St Leonard's in Fife. Coming from a background with liberal sympathies, she was interested in political issues early in her life, and in fact, along with her mother, she was active as a Liberal in the Women's Liberal Association in Harrow. Her father taught in the area, and when he retired in 1905 to Cumberland, Marshall established a Keswick branch of the National Union of Women Suffrage Societies. That group was always, in comparison with the openly militant Women's Social and Political Union, steadily constitutionalist in its methods and aims.

Her interests in the years immediately before the war, then, were primarily in campaigning to obtain the vote for women; Jo Vellacott points out that 'her outstanding achievement was in connection with the Election Fighting Fund'. She rose in the ranks of the NUWSS, that organisation having considerable impact on attitudes to the subject as the war rolled into view. On top of this activity, though, she was increasingly involved in demonstrations in support of peace, and she took part in a peace rally held at the Kingsway Hall on 4 August. Being sympathetic to the Liberal party's policies, she saw the Liberal government's lead into the war as a blow to her allegiance; Jo Vellacott makes an important point about how the war impacted on Marshall and her class: 'Such a family as Marshall's experienced major and minor traumas: the departure of this and that young relative to the war, the postponement of plans to travel, and anticipated serious drop in income … Not all small things when you add them up.'

When conscription arrived, she, along with many of her class and generation, saw quickly that there was a role to play in the resistance. She was already in the Women's International League, and so when the NCF was formed she felt drawn to further participate. Her talent was recognised and she soon found that she had a brief to create a political committee. She had an established track record in lobbying and speaking; she was an excellent communicator, and clearly she had a talent for being noticed and for influencing others, drawing them to her cause.

She gathered a team for the political wing of the Fellowship, including H. N. Brailsford and James Middleton. Brailsford had been an ILP member since 1907, had worked as a journalist, and significantly, had been part of the Carnegie Endowment for International Peace which had been detailed to report on the wars in the Balkans in 1912–13. He later wrote books on these experiences.

As noted earlier, from mid-1916 and into 1917, she stepped in to take more responsibility in the NCF, after the imprisonment of its main leaders. She showed a high level of empathic involvement in that situation, with Bertrand Russell and others suggesting that there was perhaps even something visionary about Marshall and her friends. She played an important part in the survival of the NCF in hard times. As Jo Vellacott makes clear, Marshall's work for the NCF was all a piece of her political activity prior to her involvement in the fight against conscription. She returned to the suffrage questions after the war. A measure of her importance and esteem regarding her work with the NCF may be gleaned from Bertrand Russell's account, in his autobiography, of going to meet Lloyd George regarding the treatment of conscientious objectors in prison. He went with Clifford Allen (the leading light of the NCF) and Catherine Marshall. When Russell himself had to face a prison sentence, he wrote to Ottoline Morrell about his probable prison stretch, continuing, 'I saw Miss Marshall and Allen and a number of the others – they were all delighted and hoping that I should get a savage sentence. It is all great fun as well as a magnificent opportunity.' If we read between the lines here, it becomes apparent that Russell and his circle in the peace movement felt a frisson of excitement at the face-to-face combat with the force of the law. Marshall was without a doubt ranked among the confidantes central to the NCF leaders: Brockway, Allen and Russell – who all figured in the previous chapter.

*

If we look for a more brazenly militant and intransigent woman in the NCF ranks, we find her in the person of Clara Gilbert Cole, who wrote *The Objectors to Conscription and War*, published in 1936. This book gives an account of her activities, and it reads at times like the memoir of a street fighter for justice mixed with a rage against the warmongers.

Clara wanted to be seen and to create a stir. She wrote in her memoir how:

> On 11 July 1915, Sunday, I went into Trafalgar Square with a linen placard bearing the words, 'Men and women of England, arbitration finally settles all wars. If at the end of a war why not at the beginning? If not at the beginning why not now? Demand terms of settlement from our Government as the German people are doing.'

Everything about Clara was striking, including her appearance. The standard portrait of her shows a fine-featured woman with rich dark hair and a strikingly large colourful hat with a triple-bow flourished on top. Her story is a remarkable one. She was born in 1868, the daughter of a bootmaker, although shortly thereafter she was left an orphan. She worked hard, setting about her working life first as a postal worker, before other work. Then she met and married Herbert Cole, an art student who studied at Manchester, and together they worked energetically for female suffrage.

When war came, she created her own dissenting organisation, the League Against War and Conscription. She began a series of polemical publications with *War Won't Pay*, published in 1916. Soon after this, her militant and very visible taste in protest led her into confrontation with the law; and, along with Rosa Hobhouse, she distributed leaflets, was arrested and then sentenced to five months in prison. Clara was always keen to write about whatever she did and saw, and she did so with the topic of her life inside: these were poems, published as *Prison Impressions*. The prison time, oddly, she saw as her only rest during the war.

In her short work on the experience of the objectors, she gathered together several short biographies and testaments all linked to the persecution of the resisters. The basis of her attitude she quoted early in the tract: 'Please bear in mind while reading these pages that the policy of the ruling classes is, and always has been, that of Catherine of Russia: "The only way to save our Empire from the encroachments of the people is to engage in a war, and thus substitute national passions for social aspirations."'

In the cause of the absolutists, Clara was relentless in her campaign to make their voices heard. She explained for her readers exactly what the plight of the absolutists was: 'The absolutists were men who refused to do any work behind the lines or at home, knowing it would only be in order to help the war or to release another man to go to the front.'

She singled out the case of Jack Gray as an instance of the extreme cruelty meted out to the absolutists. In a letter from a Quaker friend, she received this report on Gray:

I have just been informed that Jack Gray was recently released from Wormwood Scrubs and returned to his regiment at Hornsea. He had been before the Central Tribunal and had refused the Scheme [the Home Office offer of work]. Upon returning to his regiment he was frog-marched, put in a sack and thrown into a pond eight times, and pulled out by a rope tied around his body; under this torture he has given in. I am told also that a squad of eight men who were put to break him in, refused to torture him further.

Another prominent woman in the NCF was Violet Tillard. H. Runham Brown wrote of her main contribution:

In the very early stages of the movement Violet Tillard became associated with us and first assumed responsibility for building up the Maintenance organisation. She remained at the Head Office until the prisoners were finally released, ready to perform any duty, however humble, and always preferring to remain out of the limelight. For a time she was General Secretary. She was sentenced to sixty-one days imprisonment for refusing to reveal to the police the printers of the NCF news sheet.

Violet was born in India in 1874, where her father was a soldier. Later, she trained as a nurse at Poplar, and at Great Ormond Street hospitals. Like most of the other women in the NCF, she worked initially for the female vote, and she had a taste of life behind bars long before her anti-conscription activities, as she was one of the women who famously chained themselves to the grille in the Ladies' Gallery in parliament, and so was given a month in prison. Prison loomed again when she refused to give the name of the NCF printer, as previously noted.

Later, Violet was to become a Quaker. A branch of that group, the War Victims Relief Committee, was working in Russia after the war. Violet died from typhoid contracted in that work, and her last days were spent in Buzuluk. She was only forty-six.

*

Alongside Violet Tillard, another major figure in the NCF was Joan Beauchamp. She was born in 1890 in Somerset, the sister of Kay Beauchamp, who was a founding member of the Communist Party of Great Britain. As with most other women in the Fellowship, Joan did some time in a prison cell – ten days in her case. It was all part of her radical concerns and her desire to actually embody militant action; this shows throughout her affiliation with the suffragette movement also. She was a formidable intellect, being one of the first female graduates of the University of London, and she also published quite widely – material ranging from poetry (*Poems of Revolt*) to two works on Soviet Russia.

Joan was there when the NCF offices were raided by police; she was a close friend of the other women at the heart of the Fellowship, and she was clearly very highly valued by all her peers. She met William Thompson, a lawyer and CO who served time at Wakefield. She wrote to him in prison, and after the war, they married. In fact, Joan was not imprisoned until 1920 – it took so long for the police to track her down and take action.

*

To Lilla Brockway, wife of Fenner, must go the credit of the conception of the NCF. It was she who suggested that Fenner write a letter to the *Labour Leader* on the subject, but in fact in the end she herself did so, as Fenner reports in his autobiography: 'As early as 1914 my wife suggested that an organisation be formed of young men determined to resist war service, and with my ready concurrence as editor, she wrote a letter to the *Labour Leader*.' After a keen response, a committee was created, and Fenner notes that Lilla temporarily acted as secretary.

There were many other women in the ranks of the COs and its supporting roles, as was to be expected for any networks of radicals cooperating in the name of individual justice and liberty. Unfortunately for the history of the COs in the First World War, one of these women was involved in a highly unusual and complicated role; her story makes us return again to the peculiar nature of espionage at the time in the work of MI5 and the police. This is the contentious case of Alice Wheeldon.

The content of the case involves that of women running safe houses for COs on the run from the law. Sheila Rowbotham is one of the few writers who have investigated these networks, and in her seminal essay, 'Rebel Networks in the First World War', she places Alice and her family within this dangerous milieu. 'Hettie Wheeldon became the secretary of the Derby No Conscription Fellowship. On a local level, she did similar work to Catherine Marshall in keeping the records of what was happening to the COs.' This work extended, however, to the harbouring of wanted men. Rowbotham notes that Derby and the Wheeldons was not the only venue for this kind of protection: 'There were places to go in other Midlands and northern towns: Leicester, Sheffield, Liverpool, for example. Hettie and Alice Wheeldon were involved also in helping men escape from Liverpool to America.'

It was inevitable, that the Ministry of Munitions would start utilising spies – in the same manner that industrial spies had been used a century before in the Luddite troubles in the North – on suspects such as the Wheeldons. This led to the standard practice of the then evolving MI5 agency, of checking on letters sent by suspected radicals. Hereby a 'crime' was defined in this way, enabling the powers existing under DORA and other legislation to put the Wheeldons in a position of real trouble.

Their particular crime involved nothing less than an attempt on the life of the Prime Minister, David Lloyd George. There were certain characters existing in the shady world of counter-espionage, and one of these was set to wait on Walton Heath to murder Lloyd George as he played golf. The decided means of murdering the great man was to fire a dart tipped with curare. The people who attempted this murder could well have been characters in a popular novel of espionage, though they were in fact conscientious objectors who mixed with a bad crowd.

The great lawyer F. E. Smith (later Lord Birkenhead) has given the fullest account of the events and of the trial of the villains. What is particularly interesting is the detection of the would-be assassins. It was a case of mail interception yet again, and the family involved, the Wheeldons, were resisting the Military Services Act, and so were catalogued on a blacklist under suspicion of dissent. The level of official suspicion was raised by an element of noticeable communist activity, with some hiding their communism under the pretence of pacifism. Alec Gordon was very much the undercover hero of the case, a man who was an 'inquiry agent' and who had infiltrated the circle by pretending to be a conscientious objector escaping some kind of trouble. His brief was to fall in with Mrs Wheeldon and her family in Derby. She was a widow, and one of her daughters was married to a key player in the plot, Alfred Mason. They were living in Southampton at the time.

Gordon's suspicions about certain activities among the

Wheeldons led to a more senior officer being called in to assist the case: Herbert Booth, who was clerk to a barrister, Mr Purcell. At Christmas 1917, Booth was in Derby, and his fellow officer was quick to create an excuse for introducing the newcomer to the Wheeldons's circle, giving him the cover of being a member of a subversive group called International Workers of the World. They were duped, and Booth inveigled his way into their confidence. Booth even said openly that his group were sympathetic to the German cause. The Wheeldons had acted as friends and confidants to a number of other objectors and political dissidents on the run, hence their growing notoriety. They soon began to talk about their scheme to kill the prime minister in the presence of the agent.

Booth started the process of arranging an interception of their mail, and it was discovered that, somewhat naively, they were writing to the relatives in Southampton using a code that could have been from a *Boys' Own* comic. The code was worked out from this sentence: 'We'll hang Lloyd George on a sour apple tree.' The coded texts barely concealed their intentions of getting hold of curare and strychnine. But so well did Booth maintain his performance that, well in the confidence of Mrs Wheeldon, she confessed furthermore to an act of sabotage committed earlier. Then came the details of the assassination attempt – 'to get Lloyd George with an air gun' as she put it. A parcel containing three phials of poison was taken, with one phial in particular having a highly lethal dose of strychnine in it; the curare was an outstandingly nasty method of taking life – put on a wound or any broken skin, it causes instant death.

F. E. Smith led the prosecution when the gang were on trial at the Old Bailey on charges of conspiring to murder and inciting Booth to commit murder. Mrs Wheeldon was sentenced to ten years penal servitude; her daughter was given five years of the same; and her husband, Mason, seven years. As Smith concluded in his account, 'What they wanted was to inflict punishment on people who would not do what the prisoners thought they ought to do.'

The real interest of the case, however, as far as it concerns the practice of intelligence work, is that it provides a very early example of a type of infiltration of terrorists from within the very fibre of the domestic order. Ridiculous as the plan to ambush Lloyd George seems, had it happened it would have no doubt compared with the Phoenix Park murders, albeit with a more famous and important victim. The story neatly illustrates Browne's note about the CID and Special Branch coming together, though what it omits to reveal is an in-depth account of Booth and his very impressive undercover work.

By the end of the First World War, then, espionage was in the hands of the War Office, an organisation that had allies in all major public services; what had effectively been achieved was a close integration of the military, naval and civil forces of the state. For the first time it had become possible to have a large number of specialist professionals who could operate simultaneously in both domestic and foreign fronts. In that broader setting, the war resisters, along with the extreme socialists and other perceived left-wing extremists, were positioned in a place of great vulnerability, one removed from treason and sedition.

*

The women in the NCF, then, occupied a number of key roles. They were most of all the foundation reserve cadre to run things when the men were locked up; then they formed an ad hoc ring of supporters nationwide who would help and protect absconders; finally they were crucial to the survival of the media presence of the movement, being involved in the press and the lobbying of government through all available channels. We may add to this their capacity as writers and reporters on prison experience, as many of them faithfully recorded what was happening to the absolutists in the prisons and camps.

Not all of these women figured in the main histories of the NCF, however, as many were 'fieldworkers' putting in the hours of work without drawing attention to their contributions to the fellowship. We know of them through memoirs and documentaries. Lady Constance Malleson is just one such woman, better known by her stage name, Colette O'Niel. Known for her liaison with Bertrand Russell, she was a writer as well as an actress, the daughter of the 5th Earl Annesley. Constance and her sister Clare were activists in feminist and pacifist groups at this time; Constance went for an education in drama, renaming herself initially to Colette Niel, and then married the actor Miles Malleson – also an active pacifist. They agreed that their marriage would be 'open' and, consequently, when Bertrand Russell met her and was immediately smitten by her charms, they became lovers.

It is in the pages of Russell's autobiography that we find out what her role in the NCF was:

> Colette and her sister were both genuine pacifists, and threw themselves into the work of the No Conscription Fellowship ... I noticed Colette in the police court, and was introduced to her. I found that she was one of [Clifford] Allen's friends and learned from him that she was generous with her time, free in her opinions, and whole-hearted in her pacifism ... when war came she spent the whole of the daytime in addressing envelopes in the office of the No Conscription Fellowship. On these data, I took steps to know her better.

Their liaison lasted around five years. Colette did write an autobiography, but it is little known. Fortunately, her friends wrote about her, particularly Bennitt Gardiner, who wrote an appraisal in which he points out that she was fictionalised in a novel by Gilbert Cannan, *Pugs and Peacocks*:

> We read of 'Matty's' strong will, independent nature and uncompromising stance around that time; her Teutonic aloofness and Nietzschean resolution; her power of attracting or rejecting men and compelling their attention. As she is said to be extremely beautiful in 1916 ... it is hardly surprising that Russell found her alluring, even at first sight in Lavender Hill police station.

*

Bennitt sums her up in these words: 'Colette O'Niel ... was proud, passionate, gay, life-enhancing, avid for admiration ... and trod the byways of freedom to their utmost limit.' In contrast, Russell saw other qualities, ones that related to her active work with the cause for peace: 'She was very young, but I found her possessed of a degree of calm courage as great as Ottoline's.' But when the two lovers split later, Russell does proffer his own small criticism: 'The fact was of course, she was very young and could not live continuously in the atmosphere of high seriousness in which I lived in those days.'

If one tries to sum up the nature of the women who were prominent in the NCF, the most valuable source available is taken from their small portraits in the 1919 memorial booklet of the Fellowship. There they are, their strong profiles showing determination and resolve – and indeed also suggesting an appetite for that 'high seriousness' that the cause required. They were all examples of what Beatrice Webb meant when she said that, in the last years of the nineteenth century, the idea of service was transferred from God to man – that is, women with brains and ambition found that in serving the community and the nation in ways which they saw as noble and morally right, they were fulfilling a certain higher cause. In the memorial booklet the editor gave a relevant comment: 'I know that in all parts of the country women have worked for the CO movement as zealously as those I have mentioned, and often with great sacrifice ... We can only thank them for what they did, but we know that it was for the cause rather than for us that they worked.'

It would be too simple to look at their contribution to the NCF's work as merely an extension of other militant or radical activity. A challenge such as a head-on confrontation with a military state demanded much more grit and resolve than a vague sense that one is doing something in general for freedom.

8

QUAKERS AND THE FRIENDS' AMBULANCE UNIT

Naturally, as the Quakers were widely acknowledged to be known pacifists, it might be expected that their treatment as COs – even of the absolutist camp – would be less severe than others. But this was certainly not the case. A letter written to *The Times* shortly after conscription was introduced highlights their fears:

Sir,

The honour of the Society of Friends has been questioned on two grounds. First, they are accused of physical fear and a desire to save their own skins; secondly, of 'peaceful penetration' for the manufacture of conscientious objectors. The first accusation is due to a fundamental misunderstanding of their attitude. Quakers are not wanting in the courage which inspires their fellow-citizens. The second is not so easily dismissed. The action of some of the extreme pacifists ... is a cause of grief and indignation to many of us ... Those of us whose inborn Quakerism refuses to be bound by any dogma – are heart and soul with our country in what we believe to be the only honourable course in line with that of the Good Samaritan.

This was from Juliet Godlee, and her letter contains an accurate summary of the complexity of Quaker attitudes to the war. It would be wrong-headed to assume that all Quakers in 1914 dug in their heels and said no to war. In fact, the situation in this context was complex. No sweeping generalisations about what the Society of Friends believe about war and violence will suffice.

Essentially, there was a split in the Society of Friends as to the right response to the war, and how the individual should act or otherwise not act. Some members saw that there was a just war in process, that violence was necessary in order that good would emerge; others kept to the traditional precepts of the organisation and acted on their conscience, resolving to abstain from any participation. According to the NCF statistics, 184 Quakers were objectors, and seventy-seven of these were absolutists; fifty seven took part in the Home Office scheme.

Research by David Rubinstein on the York Quakers and on national meetings and general participation throws light on the nature of this Quaker element in the CO movement. His summing-up states plainly, that 'while majority opinion opposed the war, [an] outspoken minority gave it passionate support'. The whole situation was a vexed one for the Friends, as the basis of their beliefs states that the individual conscience will dictate reasoning and feelings. Therefore, there had to be a certain latitude in respect of whether or not Quakers who went to war should be condemned or not. Rubinstein makes reference to the letters written to the Quaker journal *The Friend* to offer some demonstrations of this dilemma:

Many of the letters to *The Friend* in the next year were sympathetic to what the writers saw as the national cause, or were at least concerned to ensure that the young male Quakers who had volunteered for the armed forces would not be disowned by the society for having done so. My calculation is that about 45 per cent of the 116 letters published in the first year of war were in favour of the war or supportive of Quaker volunteers, 38 per cent against and 17 per cent neutral or indecisive.

The leaders of the Society in various places naturally spoke out, feeling it to be their duty to explain the split in attitudes and to clarify the sources of discontent and division. Harold Capper Hunt, for instance, in defending a friend, wrote, 'If the Society stands for one thing more than another it is for liberty of conscience, and I am glad to say that in this crisis many members are at one with the British cause.'

One of the larger ironies of the Quaker situation in 1914 was that the Industrial Revolution had created a number of wealthy Quaker industrialists, their class therefore possessing a vested material interest in war, in many cases. A typical example is that of Rowntree's chocolate manufacturing works in York, owned by a Quaker family. But there was much local support for their pacifism, with a tacit indifference to their capitalist status. In contrast, and reflecting this ambiguity, a feature in the local paper proudly told its readers that almost two hundred Rowntree workers had volunteered for the forces in 1914.

At the Yearly Meeting in London in May 1915 there was a certain element in the assembly who agitated for Quaker fighters in the war to be disowned. Prolonged discussion came to the sensible conclusion that an act of disowning these Friends would effect a terrible split in the whole organisation; there were 259 Friends fighting in the armed forces at the time of that meeting. A letter of support to the fighting Friends was written; Rubinstein makes the point that this document was naturally seen as a 'manifesto' of the pro-war Friends. There were over 2,000 names on it.

Regarding Friends' experiences at local tribunals, an example from Lincolnshire will suffice to show the usual tendency. A committee was set up to support those who had to face tribunals, with one report summing up the basic problem: 'The hearings were out of keeping with the difficulty and the seriousness of the task; the objectors were treated with scant attention by the Court and offensive remarks were made by the members of the tribunal ... which had to be borne by the objectors without protest.'

There is ample evidence that the Quaker war resisters had a hard time at the tribunals and in prison, as with COs of other categories. In those areas where helpers and visitors put words on paper about the subject, we know something of that prison experience as well as the general attitudes at the tribunals. The latter were often fair in regard to Friends standing before them. Researchers have shown that the first Quaker to appeal a tribunal decision was Henry Burtt of South Kesteven, closely followed by Edward Baker. Katherine Storr has described their experience thus:

> The Friends' meeting supported his stance by deciding that he must not, under any circumstances, allow his conscience to be ruled by the military. Edward William Allan Baker ... worked for Henry Burtt's father. He made the same appeal. On the outbreak of war his job as a nursery gardener came to an end so he went home to Folkestone where he helped with the arrival of Belgian refugees ... However, his health broke down ... his religious convictions were

such that he had refused even to drill with broomsticks while at college. Both Brandon and Burt were granted exemptions, but on condition they took work of national importance.

Prison was a rather different matter. There were many COs in Lincoln prison, for instance, and the local Bishop, Edward Hicks, was very much aware of their predicament. Hicks wrote in his diary explicating upon a letter he wrote to *The Times*, on 4 April 1916,

> As I read of the handling of conscientious objectors by some local tribunals, I am visited by some painful fears ... The will or capacity to take an enemy's life is not the only element in good citizenship ... Is the nation, in its military zeal, slipping into the old vices of intolerance and persecution? Conscience is a sacred thing.

In the letter, he had written, 'It is perilous to trample on conscience; we must not try to deprive the honest objector of the protection secured to him by the law of the land.' It is significant that Hicks tried to visit Brockway in Lincoln – the prison at the very heart of his diocese – and was refused admission.

Bishop Hicks was very much involved in the struggle to alleviate the conditions of the absolutists. On 24 May 1917, there was an important debate in response to Lord Parmoor's question on the treatment of the objectors in prison. Parmoor was Charles Cripps, a Labour man, but he had switched from the Conservative Party. He was a distinguished scholar at Oxford, and a fellow of St John's. In 1917 he was a veteran with vast parliamentary and legal experience, having been Attorney General previously in 1895. Parmoor was active in a number of good causes, fighting for justice and fair play. One typical example of this is his leading of a group to ascertain any compensation due for people who had been victims of the Zeppelin raids. Another celebrated involvement was in the case of the vessel *Zamora,* in 1916, relating to the rights of ships' owners when a neutral cargo ship had been requisitioned. He had become a peer in 1914. When Hicks went to the House of Lords to support Parmoor, the pressing issue concerned the injustice of objectors being imprisoned twice for, in effect, the single offence. G. R. Evans, the biographer of Hicks, sums up the issue:

> They were being court-martialled again, sent to prison, each time with twenty-eight days of solitary confinement to serve at the beginning. It was not surprising that some of these men had suffered breakdowns and worse – 'lunacy has been caused by punishment of this kind' [Hicks's words].

Parmoor pointed out that the official argument, that such COs would be released and would then spread sedition, could be counteracted by measures allowed under DORA. But Parmoor and Hicks were up against prevailing attitudes that wanted to have all war resisters interned as alien enemies.

*

By 1917 a survey showed that 560 men from the Friends were then in the forces; 1,020 had been given exemption by the tribunals and 86 were absolutists. In the last months of the war the number of Friends in the forces had risen to 1,200. Of course, Quakers participated in all kinds of ways when it came to playing a part in dealing with the sufferings of the pacifists. In Lincoln prison, for instance, where some of the main resisters were kept (including Fenner Brockway, as described earlier) there was a Quaker chaplain, Wilfred Smith. A historian of Lincoln Quakers wrote of him, 'He and his wife Frances gave them [the COs] help and hospitality, and Frances, knowing the grimness of the conditions they had been under, made sure there was always warmth and a welcoming fire to greet them when they were released.'

The natural complement of agreeing to participate in the war by other means was to work in medicine, and the Friends' Ambulance Unit was formed. The idea for this was conceived very soon after the first Meeting for Sufferings of the Society, on 7 August 1914. It was a typical case of an amateur unit being formed in spite of the state-sanctioned provision of the armed forces. But they were soon in urgent demand, after the massive casualty figures following the first major engagements of the conflict which so overwhelmed official military resources. As a feature written by the Peace Pledge Union explains, the first initiative made by the FAU was extremely courageous: 'Early in September the first training camp took place at Jordans in Buckinghamshire, of about sixty young men ... The FAU was provided with equipment and supplies, and a party of forty-three, led by Philip Baker and including Corder Catchpool, left for Belgium.'

They were in action even before they landed in France. A cruiser was sinking after being torpedoed, and the FAU men went to work. They took the rescued men back to England, and then set off again for France. After that, the FAU continued to expand, with trains and ships following the first assemblage, which consisted primarily of road vehicles.

A typical non-Quaker recruit was the Lincolnshire man, Arthur Butler. His FAU application form survives, showing that, in 1918, when he was just eighteen, he explained himself well – writing in reply to the question of his relation to the Society of Friends,

'Although not a member at present, I have been connected with the Society of Friends since I was seven, both my parents being members (Lincoln meeting).'

At the York Monthly Meeting of the Friends, as Rubinstein has recorded, sixteen members were in the FAU and thirty were doing work of national importance.

The experience of working in the FAU was horrendous. We have ample testimony from doctors who worked in the theatre of war, including some eminent men. The writer, Somerset Maugham, for instance, described the kind of situation that stretcher-bearers could find themselves in:

> The chairs had been piled up in one of the chapels and the floor covered with straw. On this lay the wounded all round the wall and in long rows, so that there was scarcely room to thread one's way between them. In the emergency there had been no time to take away any of the emblems of religion ... Everyone who was not too ill smoked cigarettes ... here and there others wandered around, looking for wounded comrades and stopping now and then to ask one about his wounds.

The FAU was outside of Army control, and that gave it the advantage of freedom of movement and the opportunity to form its own modus operandi, though of course it was always subject to the provisionality of events and had to learn to continually adjust to the quick-changing circumstances of war. There were almost 1,200 objectors working within the FAU and we have ample testimony to the work they did in memoirs and interviews.

Corder Catchpool, who wrote a memoir of his prison experience, also left plenty of information about his work with the FAU. The first impact of Army life in France, and of the terrible conditions under which the aid and treatment services had to work, made a strong impression on him.

> I shall never in my life forget the sights and sounds that met us. Figure two huge goods sheds, semi-dark, every inch of floor space covered with the flimsy French stretchers, and on each stretcher a wounded man, desperately wounded nearly every one. The air heavy with the stench of putrid flesh, and thick with groans and cries. Four hundred wounded ... Half dead as we were with fatigue, we flung ourselves into this work throughout the night, the need was so great.

Similarly, from a nurse, Rachel Wilson, we have this account of the demands made on these volunteers when conditions were at their worst:

> The noise was deafening and one could hear the shells whizzing through the air while the boom of our guns made a background of sound ... After a bit I groped my way to the door and looked out at the blue glare of light outside ... after about ten minutes the cracking and whizzing of the shells died down and only a more distant booming could be heard.

The chairman of the FAU is on record as saying, 'They desired to stand beside their friends who went to fight, and share their dangers, devotion and sacrifice.' At the heart of the initiative was Philip Noel-Baker, who won the Nobel Peace Prize in 1959. He made an appeal for volunteers, and the response brought a good supply of people, who of course had to be trained. Just as the young men of Kitchener's new army had to go to camp and learn the elements of soldiering, so the volunteers for the FAU went to camp – in this case Jordans in Buckinghamshire.

Jordans, a village near Chalfont St Giles, has been a centre for Quakerism since the seventeenth century; such is its importance to the Society that William Penn, founder of the Province of Pennsylvania, is buried there. Old Jordans, a farmhouse, became the focal point of the training for the FAU. The actual Meeting House in Jordans is very old, reaching back to 1688, and is today conserved virtually in its original condition. With records dating back to the seventeenth century, the site enjoys a venerable status among the Friends; in 1914 it was the ideal location for a camp, with unused tracts of land in countryside being ideal for the kind of preparation for the national mobilisation of war – albeit in a supporting role in this case.

A feature in *Berkshire and Buckinghamshire Life* explains that, 'By early September 1914 the first volunteers were training at Jordans, camping in the orchard while studying stretcher drill, first aid and sanitation. Physical training featured country marches to Reading, playing a football or cricket match, before marching back,' a tennis lawn providing further scope 'to harden the muscles and stiffen the backs of those habituated to life in the office'. Noel-Baker made his office in a granary at Old Jordans farmhouse.

The FAU motto was 'Go anywhere, do anything.' They were not alone, as the Red Cross worked with and supported them. They had to give inoculations, supervise sanitary arrangements and even set up orphanages. The workers needed rest and support just as the combatants did; but whereas an officer, needing rest from the front, might have a few weeks at the Army School, where he would be refreshed regarding basic skills, the FAU volunteers had to establish their own recreation rooms, just as the YMCA had done in support areas. Again, as with the Army, the emphasis was on tea, talk, rest and books for borrowing, along with concerts of singing and comedic sketches. The main centre for this was known as the Pig and Whistle – which incidentally was not exactly in a safe area, being bombed at one time.

Individual stories of the work carried out here add a human dimension. The same issue of *Berkshire and Buckinghamshire Life* includes John Smithson's remarks on his father Michael's experience, '[He] was soon driving an ambulance on the front line. He worked for the unit throughout the war, also serving on a hospital ship and an ambulance train. In 1918 he came to work at Jordans itself, where the FAU had a convalescent home in the Mayflower Barn, so-called due to the possibly true story that it is built from the timbers of the pilgrim ship, *Mayflower*.'

*

Medical deployment in France was not the only element in the Friends' involvement in volunteer war work. There was the matter of home relief as well, as so many segments of the social fabric were under stress and threat. One special aspect of this was the large German population. Just a few days into the war, Stephen Hobhouse, who had worked with Fenner Brockway and others on major projects relating to CO activity, brought up the subject of the German population. A Foreigners in Distress Relief Committee was created, later to become the Friends Emergency Committee. The plight of the German inhabitants of Britain was such that they may have been rendered totally destitute by the hostile circumstances. Many others were interned, of course.

In an atmosphere of spy mania and crazed xenophobia, which worsened after the sinking of the *Lusitania* by torpedo in early 1915, Germans – naturalised Germans in most cases – were victimised and abused. In London alone it is recorded that there were 30,000 German people. A common quandary was that of British women who had married German men and so had lost their UK citizenship as a result. They needed homes and support, in which case the FEC worked to secure those affected jobs by creating an employment register. They had little trouble locating the people in need, and large numbers came to St Stephen's House in Westminster for help.

We have some idea of the importance of St Stephen's House in an archive of material from Anna Braithwaite Thomas and others, in which she quotes a poem by an anonymous client:

> St Stephen's House, oh, band of Quakers,
> Helping the desolate and poor,
> May God reward you for your kindness,
> To an outcast of war!

Members of the FEC also took it upon themselves to try to visit other internment camps, to check on alleged abuse and maltreatment. All this is a perfect example of what could be achieved by the Society of Friends in the First World War had they been given the freedom to be involved in these initiatives. Sadly, too many were to spend the war years condemned as absolutists, behind bars or in the settlements.

*

We need to place the work of the FAU in context. It was one part of a truly gargantuan effort from all quarters to provide health care and medical emergency assistance. As the lists of casualties grew, another resource was in demand: the back-up services of nurses and drivers, general carers and other transport and provisions people. Among these, Harrogate has one undoubted star, one who started her distinguished career as a YMCA driver and general help in February 1916. This was Betty Stevenson, who was born in Clifton, York, in 1896. At fourteen she was sent away to boarding school in Surrey, and from there to Brussels. Her father, Arthur, was a solicitor. For family reasons they were moved to South Shields, but just before the war they moved to Harrogate, where Arthur switched work to try his hand at estate agency. He evidently did well, because his home was to be Grey Gables in Cavendish Place, a notably impressive building in the Arts and Crafts style.

The family supported the work of the YMCA. This organisation by the time of war had four bases in Yorkshire, with sixty-eight workers. The working of the association was rather similar in spirit to the London settlements for the poor; students participated, and it fulfilled that great ideal of service to others which was inspiring many in the middle classes in the generation born in the 1880s and 1890s. When the war demanded much more of them in the military camps, fundraising accelerated accordingly.

After all, this is a British affair we are describing, and that being so, the cheeriness went as far as amateur dramatics wherever possible, as this letter from Frank Isherwood shows:

> We went yesterday to see the Fourth Division Follies, they are a party of Pierrots got up by the motor ambulance people. The first part of the performance consisting of songs in the 'folly' manner … In the interval, one of them came in front of the curtain and told stories. One of them was about the Bishop whose wife wrote a book and also had a child and when a gushing lady complimented him about the child he thought she meant the book

and said, 'Wasn't it clever of her – she did it all by herself, she got no help from me and certainly no help from the Archdeacon!'

Clearly, the whole enterprise of voluntary work was not only to treat the troops but also to cheer them. This was surely one of the great success stories of the war – note the idiom, 'got up by the ambulance people'. A key part of this support network, the YMCA expanded rapidly in these years; in 1918 there were fifty-five YMCA huts in Yorkshire. Betty's biographer explains how the organisation worked as the war developed:

> The YMCA followed troops to the front line and to the sites of conflict scattered across the globe – for this was truly a world war. As the wounded returned so the YMCA found itself working alongside the Royal Army Medical Corps in hospitals and convalescent homes, and in helping relatives to visit their sons. It also began to provide for the thousands of munitions workers housed in camps scattered around the country. By 1917 the YMCAs were responsible for 150 munitions workers' canteens serving *c.* 200,000 workers daily.

Betty Stevenson was an ideal candidate for a worker with such an outfit. She was energetic, resourceful and courageous. When her aunt went out to the front in early 1916, Betty wanted to follow, and she did. The work was not paid, and YMCA workers were volunteers in every sense; they were alongside the Voluntary Aid Detachment nurses, essential factors in the support network behind the fighting men. For Betty, this meant that she would need to buy a car, and at a price of £150, using money raised in Harrogate, she bought a Ford. Her mother, Catherine, joined in as well, and took a shift when her daughter was back home. From their records of experience, we gather a great deal about their work. In many ways, the demands were similar to the later WVS, when women served abroad, often at the front line or close behind. One serviceman summed up their role as 'Mother, sister and girlfriend all in one girl!' We sense that Betty was in exactly those roles in France, although in the main she was a driver for everyone.

Catherine's description of their workplace speaks volumes about the conditions and the desperate need for the YMCA to be over there: 'It stood for home, and the decencies and amenities of home, and we knew it, and it helped us keep going. I know it can be said of countless YMCA huts all past these four and a half years, that they were little lifeboats in a vast sea of warfare.'

Betty's role as driver is defined by K. V. Yapp:

When a man was so dangerously wounded that his life was despaired of, a message went through the War Office to his wife or mother indicating the fact and promising a permit to enable them to visit the hospital where the man was lying. The War Office form stated that on reaching France the YMCA would look after them. Our motor cars met every boat at Boulogne and Le Havre ... Sometimes a long motor run could be accomplished in a few hours, whereas on French railways under war conditions it might have taken days for them to reach their destination.

Betty was based at Etaples, which was where Vera Brittain more famously worked as a VAD nurse. But, as with Vera, Betty too was a writer. She wrote letters home, telling accounts of her surrounding conditions. In one such instance, 'There was an air fight here yesterday, and a Taube brought down. A piece of our own Archie shell fell outside the YMCA hut, an enormous piece

... Could you send me a pair of thick rubber gloves, size 7, [for] ladies. My hands are getting into the most fearful state with messing with the car.' Betty lost her life in France, in an air raid. *The Harrogate Herald* carried this account of her death:

> She had been busy all day ... and later with the refugees at the station. Owing to a car breaking down a group of workers were later than usual in starting off to – where we have been sending our ladies recently to sleep, for greater safety. A very early raid sent us all to the cellars and after it was over we put the party of two ladies in two cars to send them out of the danger zone, in case the planes returned. We were held up half way, and a second raid came over, forcing us to take shelter under the banks by the side of the road. Everything went well until an enemy plane, just as the raid was finishing, dropped several bombs in open country near us, probably in order to get rid of them before returning. One bomb killed Betty instantly and wounded two other workers, who are in hospital. I was by her side within a minute of the bomb falling, but nothing could be done. She could not have felt it, as she was shot through the left temple. She was taken to hospital at once.

This raid at Etaples was incredibly destructive and frightening. In nurse De Trafford's diary, she records the details she received of it in her hospital in Lancashire: 'The raid took place on Whit Sunday. On the following Friday, Etaples was bombed again ... The St John's Brigade Hospital (which was untouched during the Whit Sunday raid) was terribly wrecked – 13 wards destroyed.'

The FAU were caught up in exactly this kind of experience, so tragically typified by Betty Stevenson's life. The whole medical support spectrum consisted of the FAU, the Voluntary Aid

Detachment, the Red Cross nurses and the Queen Alexandra's nurses.

Another typical example is the case of Dr Hilda Clark, who went out to France in November 1914 with a team of doctors, nurses and a medical student, along with drivers and other assorted support staff. Clark was in charge of the whole organisation, and even planned a hospital, to be built at Sermaize-les-Bains; she kept a diary in which we may grasp some idea of the huge task ahead of the Friends, as in this extract:

> There are less than 30,000 people left in the town now, out of 120,000, and the whole place is shattered and shuttered – like a city of the dead ... How stifled by lies and hatred one feels, especially in the news from England ... If one did not feel so entirely remote from the earth it would make one very homesick. I sometimes wonder if one will ever really feel anything at all, or always be numb. The saving mercy I find in the companionship of such splendid people as we have working here.

The FAU had to turn people away by 1917. Those war resisters who were not Quakers obviously saw medical service as a fulfilling method of otherwise contributing to the war without a possibility of being involved in taking a life. One such resister was Eric McNeill, whose war experience has been assembled and published by his daughter, Heather Walker. The letter he received from the FAU in June 1917 displays the dilemma of those in Eric's situation:

> Your application to join the FAU was considered by the committee at their meeting yesterday and it was decided to accept you for work of national importance, other than ambulance, subject to

the consent of the tribunal or military authorities. The ambulance section is now full, and as you are not a Friend there would be difficulties in getting you to France.

There are few more explicit and telling statements of the impasse that many COs found themselves in when it came to finding an alternative to soldiering. McNeill, born in London in 1894, had previously been a member of an Officer Cadet Training Corps, and had truly examined his conscience. He had then turned his self to try to achieve a genuine status of a war resister. The system was against him. This was a very common situation, and of course, through the eyes of many tribunal members, it would seem as though the person sitting in front of them, waiting for a decision, was merely trying a desperate measure, with his back to the wall.

*

Concomitant to the Quaker involvement in the war, the establishment of the Northern Friends Peace Board contributed a major aid. Barry Mills gave a talk in Manchester on 21 September 2013 which offers a useful assessment of the achievements and limitations of that group. In so doing, he includes some broader comment on matters of general Quaker actions and reactions towards peace campaigns. After observing that the Boer War created a similar range of mixed reactions to that of the First World War, he goes on to make a strong case for looking to the background of the nineteenth century in order to understand those mixed responses in 1914. He notes that 'Quakers had been influenced by the Evangelical Movement and many believed that Quakers would attract large numbers of new members in an age of developing science, as they believed in the experimental approach.'

He was also critical of problematic viewpoints: 'Many Quakers had become elitist in their approach to peace work and the most serious problem was that they were not communicating a clear peace message either to fellow Quakers or to society in general.'

In this survey of the work of the Friends, Mills is helpful in selecting those people who were truly influential when it came to war resistance. He defends both John Graham and Edward Grubb, who were members of the NCF, and writes of Graham, 'He was a major inspiration for establishing NFPB and he was active with Manchester Friends at the outbreak of war in attracting crowds of up to 800 concerned citizens to the meeting house.'

The NFPB undoubtedly had a major impact on war resistance: Mills makes it clear that the organisation had members skilled in mediating ideas, noting that 'Every board member in 1913–14 was involved in speaking at or organising peace meetings. George Prior for instance visited all those in authority in the North East.' There was a special committee also for distributing literature, and a poster campaign, promoted along with a peace caravan. In modern terms, they were skilled networkers; the board formed links with similar groups across the north and they were fully apprised of the issues involved in the treatment of the absolutists. The board had a Leeds office of course – very close to the prison at Wakefield where many absolutists were kept.

Mills does also offer a critique in his analysis. He points out the failure of the diplomatists, those acting or not acting within the broad base of international European relations in the years before 1914. He contrasts the Quaker with the pragmatic realpolitik of the era: 'The Quaker call for understanding, trust and honesty in foreign relations may seem unrealistic, but the opposite traits of animosity, fear and deceit which in fact prevailed were disastrous and ultimately destructive and self-destructive.' Regarding the Quaker failure to influence other churches, Mills is aware that such a feat would have been impossible, the reason being that, as Joseph Rowntree succinctly put it, 'Organised Christianity seems at times to encourage the idea of a merely tribal deity by emphasising national differences' and that the Quaker view 'cuts at the root of militarism by the value it gives to the humblest individual.'

9

THE BEST-LAID PLANS:
CONSCRIPTION FAILS IN IRELAND

In the first months of 1916 the stresses and strains on the British government came from all directions. After two years of intense concentration on the human and logistical efforts of running a massive campaign on several fronts, to the high command and to the politicians who were striving to support them it must have seemed that problems were multiplying. One huge challenge consisted in dealing with the well-being of the troops. Not only were there a number of illnesses proliferating about the battle zones – everything from trench foot to fever, from sexually transmitted disease to the ever-present mental fatigue and shell shock – but now there was a mounting domestic drug problem.

Malcolm Delavingne, at the Home Office, was well aware of the dangers of cocaine being used by a number of soldiers on leave in London. He sent a note to his superiors that morphine was nothing compared to the use of cocaine. There was even a fear that drugs were being used as part of foreign attempts to subvert the integrity and morale of the British Army from within. Richard

Davenport-Hines, in his history of drugs, mentions one notable instance of this:

> During 1917 the English author Beverley Nichols was sent by the War Office to act as an agent provocateur of pacifists and defeatists at the Cafe Royal in Regent Street. His effeminacy aroused the hostility of vice policemen, who raided his rooms to search for drugs and question his landlady about male visitors.

With reference to the wider context, Davenport-Hines also points out that under the aegis of DORA, action against the use of cocaine could be effected. Under regulation 40B of DORA, the supply of drugs to the troops was defined as a serious criminal offence. Delavinge further convinced the War Office that there was a genuine threat from within posed by such drugs, when he wrote, as Davenport-Hines summarises:

> As Delavingne explained, regulation 40B 'was not based on an assumed prevalence among the general population. It was an emergency measure based on the known evil existing among, at any rate, a section of the troops.' The evil was believed to be a spreading evil.

This case study goes some way to explain the situation that led to another Military Service Act, and the second wave of conscription. The fact is that the government was aware that there was an approaching crisis with regard to the overall military resources needed to continue the war. Looking across the condition of the forces on active service, it would have been a simple matter to see that morale was at a low ebb; the war had become a war of attrition with heavy losses; new methods of technological and biological warfare had been introduced, to devastating effect; and now there was an increasing problem of the welfare of the men.

We could add to this, now that research into this most sensitive facet of the First World War has been undertaken, the incidence of death sentences passed and executed on servicemen. Anthony Babington has looked into this subject thoroughly, and he gives several instances of such death sentences. In 1916, at the height of this tense and worrying situation for the top brass, when morale and determination were paramount in all cases, Babington has shown that there were ninety-five executions in the British Army: ninety-three in France and Belgium, one in Gallipoli and one in German East Africa. Babington makes the point that, when men were urgently needed, corners were cut. He quotes words from a committee which had been set up to study shell shock: 'Many recruits were passed into the Army who were quite unfit to withstand the rigours of a campaign or even, in many cases, preparatory training.' As *The Sunday Independent* featured, in May 1992, 'After the war, the Army Council set up a committee to examine the executions, but its report was never published.'

*

There was also the universal problem presented to the male population – that of the overhanging sense of shame, the emasculating 'white feather' mentality. One provincial newspaper exhibited a classic example of the kind of social stigmas and judgements that tended to appear in this situation, deflecting the issue through a rubric of who had or had not attested for enlistment under the Derby Scheme:

In Leeds, the proportion of married men to single men who have attested is as two to one, and not many more than half the single men have come forward. Of those single men who have attested, it is computed that at least fifty per cent did so in the hope that they would be relieved from service as men engaged in reserved occupations ... Thus, out of the several thousands of Leeds young men who are in the four groups called up for service next month, more than half of the number have appealed to the local tribunal for exemption.

When these men had signed their short service attestation form, the small print had read:

Oath to be taken on attestation ... I will be faithful and bear true allegiance to His Majesty King George the Fifth, his heirs and successors, and that I will, as in duty bound, honestly and faithfully defend His Majesty, his heirs and successors, in Person, Crown and Dignity against all enemies and I will serve and obey all orders.

They had also signed for the duration of the war and also to agree to these words:

If employed with hospitals, depots of mounted units or as a clerk, etc., you may be retained after the termination of hostilities until your service can be spared, but such retention shall in no case exceed six months.

With these terms established, further conscription was soon considered.

On 23 March 1918 the War Cabinet had their meeting. It was held in a state of emergency; the emergency of the day was the manpower problem. There were men standing by – 5,000 officer cadets and 88,000 infantry on leave, for instance – but on the other hand there had been immense losses in the theatre of war in Europe. Over the previous two years, the government had failed to coerce the objectors, and the tribunals, with their exemptions, had proved to be a constant headache for the hard-pressed field command always in want of more men. Temporary exemptions, which were a way out of tricky ethical problems for the benches running the tribunals, had been a common occurrence, and that again slowed down the process of gathering fresh men for service, coerced or otherwise.

There was also the issue of the government promise to not send teenagers out to the front – at least, not eighteen-year-olds. But even in those early months, it was clear to the high command and to the politicians that the human resources available under the original terms were insufficient, if the struggles ahead proved to be as demanding as they were deemed to be.

In that meeting in March, the pledge concerning eighteen-year-olds was erased. That showed utter desperation. The statement given was simply that the emergency which had always been expected 'had arisen.' The man who had the unenviable task of boosting manpower was Sir Eric Geddes, at that time the First Lord of the Admiralty. The other members looked to Geddes to come up with some ideas about raising men to fight. It was he who advocated raising the age limit, and he who claimed that he could raise 300,000 men that way. But then came the topic of Ireland. Viscount French, who was in command of the forces at home, considered that Ireland would be fertile ground for recruitment.

A few days after that meeting, Lloyd George spoke with the Chief Secretary of the War Cabinet, H. E. Duke, and then to General Byrne of the Royal Irish Constabulary. His response, in the words of two historians of the Irish attitudes, was cool: 'By passing and enforcing such a measure, both the whole of the Catholics and nationalists in Ireland would be united against the British Empire ... He claimed that there would be the greatest difficulty enlisting men, that there would be riots, and he was very doubtful what the worth of the recruits would be.'

A memorandum was then put before the War Cabinet, insisting that conscription in Ireland could be enforced, but only with the greatest difficulty. Violence in the streets was predicted, along with industrial strife. There would also be the problem that, should such problems arise, British soldiers would then be needed in large numbers to suppress the trouble. As for the Chief Secretary, Duke, he was more confident that the conscription plan would work out. The press reflected the breadth of the debate. 'An Irish Officer' wrote to *The Times* expressing the opinion that, if conscription had been applied before the Easter Rising, things would have been very different;

> It may startle some of your readers to read my statement that if the British Parliament had included Ireland in the conscription bill at the start you would have had no rebellion in Ireland ... The only time I was ever interrupted in any recruiting meeting in my area was the constant call, 'Why don't you make the farmers' sons go enlist?'

There was more to it than that. Lloyd George could see the immense problem that lay before the Cabinet and its proposed legislation. The new Military Service Bill had the grandiose and ambitious aim of raking 555,000 men from Great Britain and 150,000 from Ireland. Duke saw the harsh reality of the application of such measures under consideration. He insisted that it would not be possible to extend conscription in any easy way. His one practical suggestion was to have a militia ballot, but the Cabinet was split and strong opinions were expressed by all. Eventually, the Chief Justice of Ireland was called in to comment, and he backed the view that said there would be bloodshed.

By the first week of April, the Bill was in force. *The Times* provided an analysis and presented the measures involved in the raising of the military age. The contentious words were, in the list of those eligible for being called up, 'Those who, at the time of the passing of the bill has attained the age of eighteen years and has not attained the age of fifty-one years, or who has at any subsequent date attained the age of eighteen.'

Then there was the decision regarding Ireland. This was the crucial wording here:

His Majesty may, by Order in Council, extend the Bill to Ireland, with the necessary modifications and adaptations ... An Order in Council may be issued to make special provision for the constitution of the civil court before which proceedings for any offence punishable by summary conviction under the Reserve Forces Act, 1882, the Army Act and the Military Service Acts are to be brought into Ireland.

As this was going into print, and opinions were exchanged in their turn, in the theatre of war there were major battles underway. Between 21 March and 5 April, the Second Battle of the Somme was in progress, and if anything was needed to remind the conscription fanatics how dire the situation was on the Continent, the facts are such as to confirm any negative assessment. The German Spring Offensive, known as Operation Michael, was in progress; they had shipped in half a million men from the Eastern Front and they aimed to batter the Allied line with everything they had – from gas to air power. Holding them was General Carey, whose first task was to help retain Amiens. The Germans also brought in the massive cannon made by Krupp, so they could fire from long range.

Through most of April, the Germans went head-on again for Ypres, marking the fourth battle in that iconic location; the desperate situation was summed up by Earl Haig in his notable memo: 'There is no other course open to us but to fight it out. Every position must be held to the last man; there must be no retirement. With our backs to the wall and believing in the justice of our cause, each one of us must fight on to the end.'

They are the words of a leader in dire need of reinforcements. But the debate of Ireland as a source of such fresh men raged on in the press. Lord Denman, writing from his club, was forthright and assured:

> First of all we must consider what our requirements for recruiting are. Certainly the most urgent is to enable sufficient trained men to be sent to France during the present campaigning season, say for the next six to eight months. Will conscription for Ireland help us with this purpose? Obviously, if only on account of the time that recruits' training occupies, it cannot do so.

He spoke some common sense. Conversely, others wrote to say that a government with the courage to push Irish conscription was the answer – as simple as that.

By mid-April, as the battle raged at Ypres, a press correspondent wrote to explain another consequence of Irish conscription:

> The fear of conscription has produced in three days a close alliance between parties and persons who have been at one another's throats

for the last three years. Mr Dillon is getting in touch with Mr De Valera and with Messrs Healy and O'Brien ... On Sunday the Bishops cautioned their flocks against impulsive action and at the same time warned the Government of the dangers of conscription.

At the very time all this was going on, Sinn Fein and Michael Collins were busy making things awkward for the British command (who were engaged in infiltrating the Republican ranks with spies). A typical Collins manoeuvre has been described by his biographer, Tim Pat Coogan:

> Sinn Fein, both as part of its general muscle-flexing, and because of the folk-memory of famine, became concerned at the war's acceleration of the flow of food out of the country and took a number of steps to reduce it. In the west, cattle were driven off grazing land and the ground was parcelled out for tillage by the local Sinn Fein Clubs. The rents were then passed on to the landlords ... the cattle-driving and ground-breaking were occasions of great local excitement.

During the conscription debate the government was sure that acts of sedition and rebellion were being encouraged in Ireland. The Unionists did all they could to mess with the government thinking on how to use the resources of Eire in the war. One of the top military staff members, Sir Henry Wilson (who was later assassinated by the IRA) tried to speak for the conscription hardliners, saying that, 'There were 150,000 recalcitrant Irishmen who are trying to shirk the responsibilities being borne by the two and a half million strong army then engaged in several theatres of war.'

At the Mansion House in Dublin there was a mass meeting in response to the conscription bill. Pledges had been written by De Valera, with the one relating to conscription reading, 'Denying the right of the British government to enforce compulsory service in this country, we pledge ourselves solemnly to one another to resist conscription by the most effective means at our disposal.' As Tim Coogan summarises, 'So far as GHQ [the Irish command] were concerned, if conscription were foisted on an unwilling people it would be tantamount to a massacre of civilians.'

With the wisdom of hindsight it must be said that the British government's publication of the conscription Bill introducing Irish manpower into the ranks was done more out of optimism than pragmatism. One of the most astonishing aspects of the debate surrounding the legislation was the utterly unrealistic sense of certainty some of the military minds evinced in their posturing and rhetoric, contrary to a topic which demanded a high degree of realism and sensitivity. The voice of hectoring militarism only works for a finite period of time.

SOME CONCLUSIONS

The foregoing biographical profiles and records of events, as the various war resisters faced their ordeals between 1916 and 1919 in particular, invite reflections concerning the impact such developments had on general attitudes and also on what we are to learn about the ideologies of the First World War period in Britain. It is hard to avoid the feeling that refusing to fight the Germans in 1914, and again, more visibly and staunchly in 1916, meant not only ostracism and abuse in many cases, but also a lasting stigma on the name and family involved.

There are many conclusions to be drawn from a study of the chronicles of conscientious objection. Primarily, these are related to the reclamation of that testimony of the CO experience which came in clusters in the immediate post-war years, but then thinned out. The Second World War brought a very different set of threats and presented in some ways a totally different situation for those who chose not to fight. But regarding the First World War context, there has been a marked increase in research interest in the last ten years, with, arguably, Cyril Pearce's work being centre stage. His database, The Pearce Register of British World War One Conscientious Objectors, has over 16,500 records of these individuals. Cyril Pearce was formerly Senior Lecturer at the University of Leeds, and in a blog written in May 2015, he explained the nature of his database, beginning with an account of his discovery of the actions of an anti-war community in Huddersfield:

> It began as an investigation into local claims that Huddersfield had been a special place during the war because of the number of COs and the extent to which they appear to have been supported. The research confirmed that the local claims were right. I should probably have left it at that but an intriguing question then hung in the air, 'If this was so, were there not other Huddersfields?'

His work was groundbreaking, and the outcome is a listing of the various categories of resisters, all alphabetically given, with a wealth of biographical information. Prior to this, in the histories and memoirs written 1919–20 there were basic lists of the men who died in prison and the men who were sentenced to death in Boulogne, but nothing which could be called comprehensive.

Cyril Pearce, in an article written for the British Association for Local History, wrote that,

> With few exceptions, studies of Britain during that war remain preoccupied with notions of a national picture based on national sources. In doing that, they perpetuate the nonsense that England, or even worse, Britain, can be viewed as the homogeneous whole or even a 'United Kingdom' which it clearly was not.

There have also been a number of books dealing with the general experience of people facing the tribunals, aided by the discovery of several archives of tribunal records, when it had been previously thought that they were all destroyed in the 1920s. These are being gathered together to form the basis of a project run by the Staffordshire and Stoke-on-Trent Archive Service, now amounting to over 20,000 entries.

One great upshot of this renewed interest in the COs and their stories will be a revisionist exercise, working in many cases from the local and regional level. With the widespread and ever increasing interest in family history in Britain now, the previously 'shameful' men from the family tree – lumped with the criminal black sheep no doubt – will be perhaps understood and their stories given proper recognition.

There are a few indispensable studies on the subject to which every new researcher in the subject should turn their attention, and Cyril Pearce calls three rightly classic texts – the books by John Graham, David Boulton and John Rae, all listed in the following bibliography.

In a broader sense, if one looks back at the work of the NCF one sees that the people involved in that brave stand against militarism did so in a context which we today find very difficult to understand – difficult for many reasons, not least the drastic difference that now warfare is decidedly technological and confrontation is distant and impersonal. A sniper in 1914 could target a man's head at a relatively close distance; he knew that he was taking the life of a man he could see and likely hear; he could see 'the whites of his eyes' as the saying goes. The new infantry of Kitchener's army were going to be asked to use a bayonet against another human being, to kill or be killed.

The COs were taking a stand against a brutish and savage form of violence, that may have been an accepted part and parcel of the British imperial military machine ever since the first moves to quash native rebellions two centuries before 1914. The military ethos behind the training in the vast camps across the land, run by the Northern and Southern Commands, was effectively that office workers, teachers, lawyers, businessmen and artisans were being trained to put down the harmless tools of their trade and pick up guns and bayonets in order to kill others. There was then no theoretical distance involved between civilian and military activity. The popular periodicals from the mid-Victorian years onward had been swimming with features on manoeuvres, rifle-clubs, the Prussian war game, the antics of the officers at public school – with the latter institutions being allowed to dominate the dogmatic imperial thinking and the German-hating that was called upon as soon as the possibility of a war became imminent.

With this proviso, the modern reader has to make an imaginative leap back to a time when enlisting in the Army meant having to do what we know now only from popular cultural narratives such as the film *Zulu*, in which the 1879 defence of Rorke's Drift was mounted by 130 British and allies against a vast army of Zulu warriors. The film depicts close-ups of fighting to the death. It highlights the futility of the killing, as the littering of bodies grows throughout the waves of attacks by the Zulu. But what it also does, if we relate it to 1914, is recreate the kind of stories that the recruits lapped up so eagerly in their magazines. Such engagement with the myth of imperial might and valour did not end in 1918 either. My own schooling, in the 1950s, involved history lessons featuring a large wall map and a great deal of land marked pink – every such spread of colour representing the British Empire; the teacher taught us of its glory through narratives, from Clive of India through to the Relief of Mafeking.

Those new armies, in their Pals' Battalions and Chums Battalions, were imbued with this potent ideology, and to stand outside all that, to see it for what it is – a patently one-sided militaristic triumphalism – is what the COs dared to do. The result was an ordeal they hardly could have imagined suffering at the hands of their compatriots.

In the process of researching the previous pages, I was always aware of the historical background behind the stances taken by various pacifists; but it was not until I read the prison biographies and the outrageous accounts of the tribunals that I became conscious of the witch-hunting and victim baiting that occurred, largely because those in power allowed it to do so. The freethinkers, who knew that there were truths fundamental to human relations, and norms to international relations, stood, like King Cnut, before the tide, but the tide against them was an engulfing ocean of prejudice and hatred. The playground and its bullies had grown into the supposed grown-up world in which, as school and parents had supposedly taught, there was room for fair play and respect for individual thought and conscience. In fact, certainly from January 1916 the word 'conscience' became a stigmatised word: it shifted from a fundamental concept in belief and in the moral fabric of communities into a kind of euphemism for moronic behaviour, reckoned to be out of bounds of common sense in the game of war the men of power pursued.

Switching standpoints to the British establishment position regarding the waging of war in the decade before 1914, it becomes clear that much of the drive to create an amateur army, and then later a conscripted army, had its roots in the aftermath of the Boer Wars between 1899 and 1902. In that conflict, the massive British forces only triumphed by sheer weight of numbers, with their enemy being little more than a settlement of sharpshooting farmers. The thought that, after that Pyrrhic victory, Britain would really struggle in any further confrontation with a larger enemy, provides several answers to our questions as to why, in the run up to 1916, the issue of military manpower caused much alarm and apprehension in the corridors of power.

Bernard Porter, who has established a research expertise on the development of state espionage and repression over the last two centuries, explains and summarised the pre-war situation cogently in his book, *Plots and Paranoia.* As he writes about the basis of the 'secret state:'

> Most of the key developments, in fact, took place between the summer of 1909 and the autumn of 1911. It was in those years that MI5 and MI6 were both born; the modern Official Secrets Act was passed; the 'D'Notice' system for vetting newspaper stories bearing on national security was devised; a register of aliens living in Britain was set up; blanket interceptions of certain categories of mail at the Post Office began; and the Special Branch was brought close to being a proper domestic counter-subversive agency on modern lines.

Porter makes it clear that by 1914 there was a perceived need, from the very centre of power, to work for a version of state security that had a character markedly different from the original vision of the *fin de siècle* discussions about simply reforming the Army on a basis of a 'home and away' system, with reservist manpower ready to replace their full time battalions on active service. For several reasons, the obstacles created in the way of conscription in 1916 were exaggerated, and the absolutists standing in opposition were smeared by the patriotic extremists in power as only so many more obstacles blocking the high road to what they saw as a ready state – a state with powers of surveillance and control over individuals never before experienced. There is no doubt that the fear of aliens within British society supplemented this way of thinking.

With the twisted logic of paranoia, the men who wanted to grind every available man into the military machine could play on fears of enemy infiltration; by a cruel suggestion or mere proximity, objectors soon found themselves outcast as enemy sympathisers – the worst kind, in fact, the 'enemy within'.

Other concluding remarks tend to gather around how the First World War has been mediated since the end of the Second World War. The general public are no doubt very well informed on topics such as the Cenotaph, Poppy Day and the medalled veterans of past years who lined the routes of the memorial parades, but in addition to this there has been an emphasis on heroic deeds, an intense interest in the accommodations of the trenches, and on the material history of the war as it was experienced by combatants. The home front has also received its share of celebration and memorial, with a stress on such topics as the 'canary girls' who staffed the munitions factories. There is no better national media opportunity than a centenary with human dimensions and heart-warming tales of human endurance, and we have had these in abundance. Yet, the stigma of conscientious objection lives on. There has been an erasure here.

There still remains to this day a glaring example of such purposeful annulment of the past, an instance of an episode in our history willed to be forgotten, to remain textless. This is the case of Red Roses Camp in Carmarthenshire. Has there ever been a more horrendous euphemism than that name? As the annals of conscientious objection show, there once was a camp there where absolutists were sent to suffer. In the period of preparation for writing this book, I contacted several historical organisations – two in Carmarthen – asking for any information about this place. I received no reply. It was in this camp that Alex Peddieson, to whose memory I dedicate this history, tried to help his suffering comrades in the midst of a terrible epidemic of influenza.

The camp has apparently been erased from history, just as families, in the main, have no wish to recall and talk about their CO ancestors. What we should be considering, as historians and citizens of the United Kingdom, is the courage of those who stood by their ethical principles in spite of intolerable duress from their communities. But so far, in a shameful chronicle of selective history and collective memory, we have chosen to leave them in the footnotes, except for a few initiatives, which have to be lauded. The most significant is the establishment of International Conscientious Objectors' Day, which is now being marked every year on 15 May. *The Guardian* contributed well to this in 2015 with a feature on Harry Millward, by Maev Kennedy. Millward was dispatched to Dartmoor, after a first prison spell in Wormwood Scrubs. He wrote to his wife, 'The unexpected has happened again. We are going to Dartmoor Prison tomorrow. We are all in good spirits but as you must know, Dartmoor is indeed a place I never in the past days expected to get there. There is some great history attached to this place.' As Kennedy points out, Millward had been 'jeered and frog-marched through the streets of his village' before that.

When I set out to research this work, and to ascertain my limits and scope with regards to what has been printed before, I could see that previous writers had been stunned by the discovery of so much in the records pertaining to communities who had expressed a degree of understanding towards CO attitudes. There was in fact more understanding in many communities than has been credited before. Cyril Pearce set the revisionist line of thought in motion, but it has to be said that in recording the work of the tribunals and the prison experience of COs, the heartening tales of resilience and bravery in the face of majority thinking has been found with some labour in the forgotten interstices of the fabric of history.

The photographic records of war resisters tell an alternative story. Percy Smith's pictures, which I described in my introduction, offer one of those rare instances of our being able to assemble a narrative in between the images. When Smith compiled his collection, it was to show the worst. His collection is without a commentary and, as far as I know, there was no written account to go with the pictures. I reproduce a selection of these photographs in my plate section.

Finally, I have to offer a reflection on what I would hope for future engagement of writers and historians with this subject. I should like to think that there will be a readership in time to come which has been aided towards a more objective reception of the experiences of COs in what was, in so many ways, a series of ordeals demanding from them the utmost courage and resolve. Only in the period around the centenary of conscription has the narrative of the COs ordeal been regarded as an important element in the overarching narrative of the First World War. I feel confident that, in years to come, there will be other discoveries to compare with my finding of Percy Smith's photographs, and that other historians will feel compelled to fill in the remaining blanks of the COs's stories.

ACKNOWLEDGEMENTS

In the first place, thanks go to Christian Duck and Eleri Pipien, the editors at Amberley. The book took some time to evolve, and Christian was the first to encourage its adoption. Thanks also to the library staff at Leeds Central Libraries, in the local history section, and to staff at Hull University Library, who helped to locate some of the primary source material, in both words and images. For certain technical information, discussions with social and transport historian, Bryan Longbone, were very helpful.

For permission to use the picture of the Friends' Ambulance Unit workers, thanks go to Melissa Atkinson and the Society of Friends. Thanks also to staff at the Harrogate Pump Rooms museum for help in acquiring the material on Betty Stevenson. Thanks also to Martin Birtle, for the material related to the attestation of Wybert Birtle, and for the illustration of the attestation form.

BIBLIOGRAPHY AND SOURCES

Note

The sources for the most enlightening information on the lives and experiences of COs are scattered throughout the archives of the United Kingdom, and consequently many studies have been local, focusing on such matters as conditions in specific regional camps or material on tribunals, demonstrations and the like. My largely biographical basis in this approach has meant that omissions have occurred, but the following listings do present a short survey of material in print. There has been a tendency for research to split into either very academic writing, or into general surveys. Biographical approaches have emerged more recently, as archives have opened up, and because the pressures of centenary revisits, as it were to this CO experience have led to revisionist thinking.

The sources for the tribunals are, unavoidably, individual testimony, and subject to bias and distortion, but taken together, there is common ground regarding the overall patterns of what kinds of processes occurred at the tribunals, with similar material in each category, from local to appeal status.

Many archives hold primary material too, but such is the

volume of printed testimony that I have confined my use of sources to these.

There is a need now, one might argue, for a full bibliographical survey of writings on the First World War conscientious objectors. It would, I feel sure, require someone with access to far more original sources than I have, but hopefully, the following will make a useful contribution to that ongoing process.

Books Cited

Primary Sources

Asquith, H. H., *Letters to Venetia Stanley* Edited by Brock, Michael and Brock, Eleanor. (Oxford: OUP, 1985)

Brockway, Fenner, and Hobhouse, Stephen, *English Prisons Today* (London: Longmans Green, 1922)

Brockway, Fenner, *The Recruit: A Play in One Act* (London: The National Labour Press, 1918)

Brockway, Fenner, *Towards Tomorrow* (London: Hart-Davis, MacGibbon, 1977)

Brooks, J. Barlow, *Lancashire Bred* (Oxford: Church Army Press, 1960)

Catchpool, Corder, *Letters of a Prisoner* (London: George Allen and Unwin, 1941)

Chamberlain, W. J., *A C.O. in Prison* (London: No-Conscription Fellowship, 1916)

Chamberlain, W. J., *Fighting for Peace* (London: No More War Movement, 1918)

Cole, Clara Gilbert, *The Objectors to Conscription and War* (Manchester: Co-operative Printing Society, 1936)

Dolby, I. E. A., (Ed.) *The Journal of the Household Brigade 1871* (London: Clowes and Son, 1871)

Duckers, J. Scott, *Handed-Over* (London: C. Daniel, 1917)

Graham, John W., *Conscription and Conscience: A History 1916-1919* (London: George Allen and Unwin, 1922)

Hobhouse, Mrs Henry, '*I Appeal Unto Caesar*' (London: George Allen and Unwin, 1917)

Pankhurst, E. Sylvia, *The Home Front* (London: Hutchinson, 1932)

Russell, Bertrand, *The Autobiography of Bertrand Russell Volume II* (London: George Allen and Unwin, 1971)

Russell, Bertrand, 'Conscientious Objectors', *Manchester Guardian* 11 May, 1917

Strachey, Lytton, *The Shorter Strachey* (Oxford: OUP, 1980)

The Queen's Regulations (London: HMSO, 1886)

Walker, Heather, *Eric McNeill, My Father* (Lulu.com, 2014)

Other Works Cited

Atkin, Jonathan, *A War of Individuals: Bloomsbury attitudes to the Great War* (Manchester: Manchester University Press, 2002)

Boulton, David, *Objection Overruled* (London: McGibbon and Kee, 1967)

Brittain, Vera, *The Rebel Passion: a short history of some pioneer peacemakers* (London: George Allen and Unwin, 1964)

Brodsky, Joseph, *Less Than One: Selected Essays* (London: Penguin, 1986)

Burnham, Karyn, *The Courage of Cowards* (Barnsley: Pen and Sword: 2014)

Canetti, Elias, *Crowds and Power* (London: Penguin, 1962)

Carey, John, *The Intellectuals and the Masses* (London: Faber, 1992)

Chesterton, G. K., *Selected Essays* (London: Wilco Publishing, 2009)

Clouse, Robert, (Ed) *War: Four Christian Views* (Downers Grove, Illinois, Intervarsity Press, 1981)

Cole, Clara Gilbert, *Prison Impressions* (London: Universal Publishing Co., 1917)

Curtis, Tony, (Ed.) *Wales at War* (Bridgend: Seren, 2007)

Davenport-Hines, Richard, *The Pursuit of Oblivion: a social history of drugs* (London: Phoenix, 2004)

Davies, Susan, *Quakerism in Lincolnshire* (Lincoln: Yard Publishing, 1989)

Drabble, Margaret, *The Oxford Companion to English Literature* (Oxford: OUP, 1985)

Evans, G. R., *Edward Hicks: Pacifist Bishop at War* (Oxford: Lion, 2014)

Fest, Joachim, *Not I: A German Childhood* (London: Atlantic Books, 2012)

Gillman, Harvey, *A Light that is Shining: An introduction to the Quakers* (London: Quaker Books, 1988)

Hayman, Ronald, *Leavis* (London: Heinemann, 1976)

Hibberd, Dominic, *Wilfred Owen: A New Biography* (London, Weidenfeld and Nicholson: 2002)

Holroyd, Michael, *Lytton Strachey* (London: Penguin, 1971)

Isherwood, Christopher, *Lions and Shadows* (London: Hogarth Press, 1938)

Jones, Nigel, *Rupert Brooke: Life, Death and Myth* (London: Richard Cohen, 1999)

Maddox, Brenda, *The Married Man: The Life of D. H. Lawrence* (London: Sinclair Stevenson, 1994)

Marwick, Arthur, *Clifford Allen: The Open Conspirator* (London and Edinburgh, Oliver and Boyd: 1964)

Maugham, W. Somerset, *A Writer's Notebook* (London: Heinemann, 1951)

Mellors, Robert, *In and About Nottingham* (Nottingham: J. & H. Bell, 1908)

Morton, H. V., *In Search of England* (London: Penguin, 1960)

Noyes, Frederick Walter, *Stretcher Bearers. At the Double* (1923)

Parini, Jay, (Ed.) *Last Steps: The Late Writings of Leo Tolstoy* (London, Penguin: 2009)

Pearce, Cyril, *Comrades in Conscience: a study of an English community's opposition to the war* (London: Francis Boutle, 2001)

Porter, Bernard, *Plots and Paranoia* (London: Routledge, 1989)

Rae, John, *Conscience and Politics: The British Government and the Conscientious Objector to Military Service* (Oxford: OUP., 1970)

Ridge, W. Pett, *The Bustling Hours* (London: Methuen, 1919)

Rowbotham, Sheila, *Friends of Alice Wheeldon* (London: Pluto Press, 1984)

Rubinstein, David, *York Friends and the Great War* (York: Borthwick Papers, 1999)

Starling, John, and Lee, Ivor, *No Labour, No Battle* (Stroud: Spellmount, 2009)

Thomas, Anna Braithwaite, and others, *St. Stephen's House: Friends' emergency work in England 1914–1920* (London: Society of Friends, 1920)

Vellacott, Jo, *Militarism versus Feminism: writings on women and war* (London: Virago, 1987)

Walter, George (Ed) *The Penguin Book of First World War Poetry* (London: Penguin, 2006)

Zurbrugg, A W (Ed.) *Not Our War: Writings against the First World War* (London, Merlin Press: 2014)

Books of General Reference

Beardshaw, Sylvia, *The Boys on the Board: Chaddesley Corbett* (Stourport-on-Severn: Chaddesley Corbett Local History Society 2014)

Davenport-Hines, Richard, *Universal Man: The seven lives of John Maynard Keynes* (London: William Collins, 2015

Dostarer, Gilles, *Keynes and his Battles* (London: Edward Elgar Publishing, 2007)

Elsworth-Jones, Will, *We Will Not Fight: The Untold Story of World War One's Conscientious Objectors* (London: Aurum 2008)

Glover, John, and Silkin, Jon, *The Penguin Book of First World War Prose* (London, Penguin: 1989)

Kerr, Gordon, *A Short History of the First World War* (Harpenden: Oldcastle Books, 2014)

Liddington, Jill, *The Road to Greenham Common: Feminism and Anti-Militarism in Britain since 1820* (Syracuse, New York State: Syracuse University Press, 1991)

Rubinstein, David, *York Friends and the Great War* (York, Borthwick Papers: 1999)

Senechal, Marjorie, *I Died for Beauty: Dorothy Wrinch and the culture of Science* (Oxford: OUP, 2012)

Smith, Lyn, *Voices Against War: A Century of Protest* (Edinburgh: Mainstream, in association with the Imperial War Museum, 2010)

Solomon, Sheldon, and Greenberg, Jeff, *The Worm at the Core: On the Role of Death in Life* (London: Allen Lane, 2015)

Townson, Duncan, *Dictionary of Modern History 1789–1945* (London: Penguin, 1994

Articles and Essays/Contributions to Collections

Anon. 'First World War Courts Martial' *Sunday Independent* 25 May, 1992

Anon. 'Nobler Cares, By George Hare Leonard' *The Spectator* 13 February, 1909 p.24

Arscott, David, 'Freelance' in *The Times Literary Supplement* 13.3. 2015 p.20

Brown, Jonathan, 'Jailed, Strait-jacketed, starved, sentenced to death – the men who refused to fight' *Guardian*, 27 May 2014 p.27

Davies, Lucy, 'Shooting Suffragettes' *The Daily Telegraph* 13 June, 2015 pp R20–1

Gregory, Adrian, 'You might as well recruit Germans' in Gregory, Adrian, and Paseta, Senia, *Ireland and the Great War* (Manchester: Manchester University Press, 2002) pp. 113–32

Fellowship of Reconciliation, Pax Christi, Peace Pledge Union, Quaker Peace and Social Witness, Women's International League for Peace and Freedom, *Opposing World War One: Courage and Conscience: an information briefing about conscientious objectors and peace activism in the First World War* (London: above groups combined, 2013)

Gardiner, Bennitt, '1916' from the *Bertrand Russell Journal*, online: www.escarpmentpress.org/russell/journal/article

Hamilton, Ian, 'Evil Days' *London Review of Books* Vol.14. No.14 23 July, 1992

Hoyt, Herman A., 'Nonresistance' in Clouse, Robert G., (Ed) *War: Four Christian Views* (Downers Grove, Illinois: Intervarsity Press, 1981) pp. 29–57

Huws, Bleddyn, 'Undergraduate to Professor in a Day' *Prom* (Aberystwyth: University of Wales, 2015 pp. 20–2

Kelly, Duncan, 'Multipliers' *Times Literary Supplement* 29 May, 2015 pp 3–4.

Kennedy, Maev, 'Poignant Stories of first world war's conscientious objectors go online' *The Guardian* 15 May, 2015

Lewis, Stephen, 'The Men of Conscience who Refused to Fight' Lancashire Telegraph 14 March 2014: online at www. lancashiretelegraph.co.uk

Mills, Barry, 'The Achievements and Limitations of the Northern Friends Peace Board 1913–1920 'Peace History Conference at Manchester 2013

Newberry, Jo Vellacott, 'Anti-War Suffragists' *History* Vol.62 Number 206 October, 1977 pp. 426–31

Our Parliamentary Correspondent, 'Military Service' *The Times*, 11 April 1918, The Times Digital Archive Web. 17 June, 2015

Owen, Trefor M., 'Obituary: Iorwerth C. Peate' *Folklore* Vol. 94, 1983 p.20

Pearce, Cyril, 'War Resisters in Britain during the First World War: an online opportunity for new research. *Local History News* Number 111 Spring 2014 online p. 5–7

Pittock, Malcolm, 'Max Plowman and the Literature of the First

World War' *The Cambridge Quarterly*, Vol. 33, No 3 2004 pp. 217–43

Storr, Katherine, 'Enlistment, Conscription, Exemption, Tribunals'

The Worker, 'Scenes at a Tribunal' 25 March, 1916 (University of Leeds: 5 November, 2001)

Internet Sources

Hansard reports:

26 June 1916 Vol. 83 cc521-8 *Conscientious Objectors*

www.escarpmentpress.org

www.forthesakeofthekingdom.co.uk

www.grahamstevenson.me.uk

www.jordansquakercentre.org

www.libcom.org.

www.library@quaker.org.uk

www.nfpb.org.uk

www.quakerstrongrooms.org/library-for-researching-world-war-1

www.warhistoryonline.com

www.watchtower.org

Archives

Anyone researching the conscientious objectors of the First World War owes a debt of gratitude to Cyril Pearce, who painfully compiled an alphabetical list of these individuals, with basic biographical details of each one.

See: www.livesofthefirstworldwar.com for access to the database.

Also, as a major source, the Peace Pledge Union website provides comprehensive guidance on the subject. See: www.ppu.org.uk

Asquith Dalton Papers: Leeds University Library GB 206
Liddle Collection: Leeds University Library CO 023

Newspapers and Periodicals Referenced

Daily Telegraph
Grimsby Evening Telegraph
The Graphic
The Times
The Yorkshire Post

INDEX